Golden Boy

Golden Boy

Karl Horst

ISBN: 978-1-4269-0082-2 (Soft)
ISBN: 978-1-4269-0083-9 (e-book)

*We at Trafford believe that it is the responsibility of us all, as both individuals
and corporations, to make choices that are environmentally and socially sound.
You, in turn, are supporting this responsible conduct each time you purchase a
Trafford book, or make use of our publishing services. To find out how you are
helping, please visit www.trafford.com/responsiblepublishing.html*

*Our mission is to efficiently provide the world's finest, most comprehensive
book publishing service, enabling every author to experience success.
To find out how to publish your book, your way, and have it available
worldwide, visit us online at www.trafford.com*

Trafford rev. 01/15/2010

 www.trafford.com

North America & international
toll-free: 1 888 232 4444 (USA & Canada)
phone: 250 383 6864 ♦ fax: 812 355 4082 ♦ email: info@trafford.com

Golden Boy

By Karl Horst

TO MY FAMILY FOR STANDING UP,
TO MY FRIENDS FOR STEPPING UP,
TO NONA FOR STAYING UP,
TO MY MUSE FOR SHOWING UP,
AND TO ME FOR NEVER GIVING UP ......
WHEN EVERYTHING ELSE WAS FALLING DOWN.

WARNING: EXTREME HONESTY

The short fiction stories are exactly that, works of fiction. Any similarity to names or character is a coincidence and should be ignored.

Contents

Contents

Chapter 1 Life

Clarity unfolds in the morning.

For as long as I can remember, writing has been my escape. It has served to be an effective means of releasing my thoughts onto an imaginary audience. At age twelve, I began compiling a journal of poetry that set the tone for how I viewed the world. Not very carefree, I agree, but I couldn't stop the words from seeking a resting place. University and adulthood could not suppress the drive to express myself through literature. I took courses in creative writing, carried a journal and the insistent voices in my head became silenced for a while. I swore to let these desires lie dormant until I was given the opportunity to write a piece about truth. Life would later force me to keep that loose promise.

As I sit on the couch with a million thoughts, I gaze down at my thin legs and groan. Too many things to say, too much to unveil and I only hope to be given the time to take you with me on this soulful journey. I am filled with an overwhelming cluster of memories. The light in the room fades and with it, my eyesight and emotional grace distort. A comforting recollection steps forward in the image of my mother.

"How do you eat an elephant?" says the blonde figure with anticipation.

"One piece at a time," I reply to the nurturing scene. The first step and first bite are the hardest to get through … so here goes.

My name is Janji Slab and I'm different. I live in South Africa, where fear is normal and joy is downplayed. It is a hard place to be when you know you are a wolf in a field of angels and devils.

I was diagnosed two years ago with a medically rare disorder, which has left me paralyzed and has no known cure or solution. The details of that discovery are not important now. The position that I find myself in, however, is that when you get sick or injured, people turn to you for wisdom, as if you are aware of the answers to all of life's questions because you already have one foot in the grave. Perhaps it's the comfort of relativity that people find when they acknowledge their problems to be not that bad in comparison to yours. If that's the case, then that's ok.

Lessons and happiness come in many forms and when they are least expected. My initial answer to the challenging hurdles before me is a poem, which highlights my path and is the structure of this novel that is written in real time. The present is what we ultimately own. Everything else is simply garnish. This is my reality, my truth. It is the fragments of my life's experiences, understood through hindsight. Although these pages relay actual events, they contain messages of rebellion against common myths. Clichés may appear true to everyone but we are unique in our search for individuality. We are the sculptors of our lives and ultimately mould our own destinies; fate simply supplies us with the choices and the inspiration.

It was not too long ago that I was faced with a choice, accept my fate, come to terms with my new limitations, or refuse to go quietly into the distance, and turn to fight for my dreams. Modern advertising makes correlations and associations between products and life. Wow! Life is the broadest category there is and our roles within it are often subject to a conscious awareness of our behavior and feelings. Please don't feel sympathy for me because I don't. The poem is called 'I am not sorry'.

POEM
I AM NOT SORRY

(For Cheri)

I am not sorry for the life I have lived,
For the dreams I have chased,
And the lenses I had selected,
To weigh my self-worth upon.

I am not sorry for the friends I have made,
For the jokes and big plans,
And the priorities that changed,
As we grew into our new worlds.

I am not sorry for the love I have given away,
For the hearts I have collected,
And the disappointment I held onto,
When the hope of an ideal was not enough.

I am not sorry for the seriousness I have felt,
For the insults that stung,
And the truth that was discovered,
In the expectation of slaying a monster.

I am not sorry for the sickness I have endured,
For the blind pleas for relief,
And the long days spent in bed,
Unable to locate the invisible spectator.

I am not sorry for the solutions I have pursued,
For the qualified assumptions,
And the blessed but fragile authority
Of those who think they own compassion.

I am not sorry for the kindness I have seen,
For the humanity that exists,
And the gentility that occurs quietly,
When the people thought no one was watching.

I am not sorry for the thoughts I have had,
For the emotions I have survived,
And I realize the necessity of these things,
That bring the calm with the storm.

I am not sorry for the fight that keeps me alive,
For the love that pulls me forward,
And all the doubts I may find,
For that, I am not sorry.

Chapter 2 Self Worth

The beginning is never the end.

Up until the time I got sick, I thought the criteria for happiness was easy. Earn lots of money, be adored by women and live by the rules of man and God. All of these things, I thought, were governed by a universal truth that we all share at all times. I believed the same to be true for hardship. It was always considered by me to be a punishment for past indiscretions or wrongdoings.

After my diagnosis, there was an abundant supply of information and suggestions as to what I should pursue to insure my survival. All I knew was that I wanted to write a book, go for a walk and help people. Going through the motions of anger, denial and acceptance, I realized some very distinct things about myself.

I did not know what type of person I was, and until I did, I could not accept my expected fate. In order to figure out what I was capable of, first I needed to know what I was made of. Like so many before me, I turned to my family tree. It was after all, my own personal history and what came out, was the first step towards my healing process and the search for self worth had begun.

I have learnt that a person is more than the sum of their parts and my inner voice could be silenced no longer. It says to me with an absolute certainty that reality is based on what you believe, not on what you have learnt. I wrote this story about my family with that in mind; and it was sent to them, via email, the following day. I used the name Karl to depict myself as it was the name given to my great-uncle. I, like everyone else, put myself at the centre of this honest universe.

SHORT STORY

THE WRIGHT WAY

Tamaryn Meikle and I

5

In the winter of 1977, Karl Wright was born and he was perfect. Even the nurses were lost in his bright blue eyes and gentle smile. His parents were middle class white citizens living on the east coast of South Africa and dreaming of a life they had read about in books or seen on TV. Karl was born six months after they were married. He was not planned, but rather, an idea whose time had simply arrived. This was ironically the first and last time Karl was ever early for anything.

Karl was an inquisitive youngster and he started learning about the world as soon as his eyes had properly opened. His father aptly named him 'King Karl' as soon as his informal education had begun. Karl's mother was a teacher at the local primary school and her input was structured and fuelled by love. She taught him language and fed his overactive imagination with constant approval and affirmation.

Karl's parents both worked, trying their hardest to avoid the tyranny of mediocrity, but as a result were forced to let Karl spend most of his days learning his own lessons and creating his own world with which to play. Karl was unusually receptive to the subtle clues that were hidden in the wind and underneath his own thoughts. He would later discover that his whole life was a series of seconds glued together by his emotions. Karl was, however, very imaginative.

The house where they lived had a Spanish design. It was a small rectangular home with white walls that were indented on the outside, resembling a large golf ball. The house set the scene for Karl's imaginary world. He could not remember when exactly it started, the memories were like broken glass that he put back together as an adult.

Karl was a day-dreamer. When he listened to his parents' vinyl records scratch and spin the sounds of The Doors, his imagination would take him to a place where he was impressive and strong. Karl's heart would pound with excitement and he would see a new world transform before his eyes. "Perhaps," he thought, "men become what they see when they dream."

Karl saw himself as older when he daydreamed. He saw his future so full of substance and confirmation, and he looked forward to his daily escapes where he would meet himself as the perfect boy again, with the perfect smile. He was golden. Karl was a seven-year-old boy waiting for his future to arrive.

When Karl played with his friends at home, he would transform into the creator of a conjured-up imaginary realm, they were the protagonists, and they were always victorious during their games. God was happy because his children were at play.

The house was modest with two small gardens on either side; the back of the property overlooked a valley, and seemed to go on forever. The swimming pool had a raised deck that had water maidens on both ends. At the bottom of the pool was a mosaic mermaid. Karl would dive down to the mermaid and excitedly swim towards her, his seven-year-old excitement contained in her mesmerizing stare. This was Karl's secret Atlantis, and she was his queen.

Karl could not stay with the mermaid for long as he was forced to resurface and breathe; this relationship would repeat itself throughout Karl's life, the pattern with every girl thereafter; alluring intrigue, a childlike excitement, followed by a euphoric sense of safety, and then an inescapable claustrophobia.

Karl's Atlantis dreams started to change, he reinvented the game and his watery maiden's role within it, but as he grew his imagination began to fade. He realized that to be victorious he had to abandon his Atlantis. "You cannot breathe down there," his parents would say, "it's time to live and be happy in the real world". Karl knew they were right, and he knew what he had to do, he had to focus his energies on the dry world. He found it ironically colder above the surface of the water; there was more noise and less peace in the dry world. Karl subscribed to the views of those who guided him. The hardest part about this new world was the weight that he saw everyone carry.

"Mermaids," Karl thought, "were so beautiful compared to these mannequins that smiled with their teeth." He coped bravely in this new place by adopting a mentality of survival. The rules were simple; be suspicious, be careful, appear strong, do not offend, be apologetic, and always be respectful. But the hardest rule for Karl was exclusive love.

Over the years Karl's music changed, but his victories were still great. He had somehow come to believe that not all dreams were attainable. He tried to change the world and fill it with tranquil water because he was determined to take the harder route in life and love, but Karl could not change the water within the pool. As an adult Karl, realized that his truth was between two worlds, and in order to find it, he would have to drain the pool.

Revelations came and went. Years passed and priorities changed, but one thing remained constant, the conflict in Karl's heart between the world he created under the water with his mermaid when he was a boy, and the world above the surface that he was forced to come to terms with as an adult. He realized that he was cut in half – his heart was unknowingly stained. He looked into his past to try to understand why he had always felt a sense of unworthiness, an uncontrollable fear linked to everything he did. Why he felt he could never live up to his own and everyone else's expectations, why he lived in constant fear of persecution and over-exposure, and why feelings of loneliness and frustration seemed to grow with every breath he took. Karl had always felt weak and misunderstood, which bred an increasing feeling of anger and a need for revenge. He lived in a continuous state of guilt, although he couldn't remember doing anything that warranted the intensity of the emotion.

Karl wanted to know why his dad always told him to prepare for the worst and why his mom was afraid of ridicule or being undermined. This seemingly simple task was harder than anticipated. People remember things the way they want to, not the way they occur. Bits of information were brought to the surface after a few Irish Coffees or during times of consolation and the pieces of glass were slowly put together in Karl's mind. He never got the full stories but they were specific enough to work with and answer his questions.

DAD'S STORY

Horst Wright was born just before the end of the Second World War. His father (Horst Senior) was a Captain of the Royal German Army and his mother was a very young and inexperienced bride living in Germany with her firstborn. The war had ended suddenly and calm had fallen over a once turbulent nation. A new addition to the Wright family was also on the horizon and at home, joyous preparations were being made. There was only one last meeting arranged by the German regime to honor their brave efforts and Horst Senior was obliged to attend. This, however, was the same day that Bjorn Wright chose to enter into this world and Horst Senior was frantically pulled from his commitments and rushed to the nearby hospital where his twenty-year old wife was to be waiting. The only non-tragic part of this story was the birth process. It was uncomplicated and smooth and Heidi Wright was discharged from the hospital even before her husband had been contacted. She was waiting for her husband at home with her two-year old son and newborn infant – excited and anxious.

Horst Senior's car did not reach the hospital. It fell into an iced lake. So as one branch of the family tree was grown, so another fell. Heidi Wright never fully recovered from this sudden tragedy. She raised her two children as best she could and remarried twice in search of the happiness she had once known. Her two firstborn children, Horst Junior and Bjorn, were taught that life was a lesson in survival and the tolerance of relative hardship. Perhaps her mind was caught in a time of innocence, but her heart was caged in grief. Horst Junior was an empathetic child who was sensitive to his mother's forcibly detached character. He realized that in order to learn his place in the world, he would have to seek comfort elsewhere. His younger brother had become a priority and without a father role model, Horst was flying blind.

Horst sought refuge and a sense of purpose in others. He could remember specific details of every story told to him by virtually everyone that crossed his path. Horst's daydreaming escapes were found in the genuine interest in other people's lives. He drifted between personal priorities: between jobs, friends, women and hobbies. What was really important to him was respect and security.

Horst found himself living in South Africa in a house with two half brothers, a jealous stepfather and a mother who was turning into stone, and so Horst worked hard to avoid all emotional turbulence that was brewing in his world. Love is always present, but seldom voiced.

One day Heidi left to return to her native land, this time, without her grown kids and her new husband. Horst had lost two parents in nineteen years. His life lesson was to carry on regardless. He swore to create his own perfect family even though he could not recognize one from his own memories.

When Horst did get married, he vowed to protect his family by giving them the things he never had. He was overcautious so that his children never felt what it was like to be unwanted or abandoned by circumstance. However, Horst continued to defend his mother's life choices through every enquiry and question from his son, Karl.

"We all want to do things, son," he said, "but most of the time we do what we have to. Just make sure that you do it the right way."

"But a wrong turn is the best way to get your bearings and survival is not enough, Dad," Karl replied, "I have dreams and I plan to implement them in the event of becoming huge." Karl could see in his father's eyes that he understood.

"I'll back you in whatever you choose to do my boy, just remember to be realistic." Karl had been pulled from the pool once again.

"Thank you, but aren't you angry?" Karl asked his father. Horst lowered his eyes as if to say "Not anymore." Karl could see that his father still carried the guilt of his past losses. Karl sat quietly with him, he wondered how his father could be so silent in the face of total honesty, he reached out and touched his dad's arm. If his hand could have spoken, it would have said: "You don't have to appear so strong, you never did have to." Horst was never intended to be Heidi's savior. The fall from that duty was always going to be too great and yet, Horst carried it around with him everywhere. Karl was no more fooled by his father's silence now as an adult, than he was as a seven-year-old child.

"Let's go inside son, it's getting dark, and it's not safe."

The two men entered the house; Karl made another Irish Coffee while his father locked every door twice. "The secure locks may have protected the family," Karl thought, "but the coffees and the people made it a home."

MOM'S STORY

Diana Wright was born Diana Viljoen, the fourth of five children in an Afrikaans family, they lived in a small town called Kroonstad. Her father was an educated, no-nonsense teacher at the small town high school. Diana grew up in a Catholic family where children were to be seen and not heard. It was in this environment that Diana found a sanctuary. Her mother was a typical, friendly and care-giving housewife; the house was filled with baked goods and communal efforts. The children played together and were taught that respect for elders was non-negotiable. Diana's father was the head of the family, and as such was perceived to be wise and all-knowing. He was not a conservative man, but rather a free-spoken, slightly rebellious authoritative figure; his wealth was gauged by his fast-growing family legacy. Diana's mother supported her man as any good woman did in a small town wrought with gossip and boredom.

The five children developed their personalities fast and Diana was no exception. As an infant she was set to be the pretty one. At the age of seven, Diana contracted polio and there was no known cure for her disorder. Isolation was the prescribed treatment for the little girl, and Diana was sent to a special school until the age of nine. She was surrounded by kind strangers, but strangers nevertheless.

One vivid memory of this time stayed with Diana forever; she was en route by train from the special school to see her family but when she arrived at the train station, they weren't there. Diana waited for them for hours under the watchful eye of the station-master. She had felt her heart break many times before, the first was when she was forcibly removed from her family, the second was when she was told she would never walk again, and finally, she was left alone on the train's platform. Eventually her parents arrived having experienced car problems. The tears had welled up in her eyes and she had felt only one sensation – what it was like to be forgotten. Her fears were allayed in the short term, but the effect was long-lasting. Diana was no ordinary little girl, her father taught her to question everything – God and men alike.

At the age of nine Diana was returned home, she continued to attend school where she excelled at provincial hockey despite the polio. Her left arm was disfigured and served as a source of embarrassment throughout her teenage years. When the children commented on this part of her anatomy, she struck back with a fierce tongue; this gave Diana a sense of power even when it was not the case. Her words were a weapon she had at her disposal at all times, the outside voices of ridicule were silenced and this allowed Diana to become the pretty girl once again. Boys became very interested in her because of her inherent strength and outer appearance and she felt that she was wearing her heart on her sleeve rather than her pain.

The pain, however, was present inside her home where Diana would see her caring parents change form daily. Some people drink alcohol to expose their inner selves, but Diana's parents drank to numb their frustrations; the children grew up and never spoke of the seemingly embarrassing trend. The small town buried their secrets, their days were filled with love, but their nights were plagued with uncertainty.

Armed with her parents' consent and her thirst for knowledge, Diana left one fine day to travel the world. She traveled in search of herself and she found a few people who resembled the life she imagined she always wanted. No man, however, could hold her down, as no man could measure up to her father's charisma. They all seemed to want something from her, which she simply did not have to give – acceptance. Diana decided she would become the ideal and she started training to become a teacher. Her intrinsic strength was testimony enough to her father's influence so she searched for a man who embodied her father's caring nature, a man who was interested in who she was, not what she did.

Diana's anger was never left alone unlike the little girl left at the train station. The anger she felt fueled her strength and ambition to succeed at all costs; it came, however, at a price, and that cost was a guarded suspicion. She learnt to portray an image of authority at all times which kept both the cynics and fearful away so she could focus her energies on raising her own children. Diana was sure not to let her own children experience any of the obstacles that she was forced to endure. She swore to protect them from those who meant them mental or physical harm. She took her father's role as the head of the family in her own home, but she could not suppress the pain and sadness she had once felt. These pains were no longer physical; they were lodged in her memories and resurfaced when activated by passing remarks. They became uncontrollable responses to external triggers. Unconditional love, she thought, was her only escape, and maybe her own family could provide that.

As her children grew, loyalty became a focal point. Diana questioned the loyalty of her friends and her colleagues while she maintained that she was happy with her place in the world. She wore her scars with pride, but children don't see pride and Karl tried to access the innocent, pretty little girl. Karl found this girl in moments of desperation when he was sick and lost, her touch was the softest he had ever known and it came without request or justification. Karl and Diana were joined in their efforts to find truth and acceptance. It was in these times that Diana believed she could carry Karl's pain, as she had kept her own contained for so long, but burdens cannot be enclosed in a glass or a thought. Burdens are to be shed and left in a time where they once had authority.

"The present is filled not with water but with pure potential," Karl thought.

At twenty-eight years of age, Karl Wright was forced to sit down and fulfill a promise he had made to himself. He had vowed to write a story unlike any other, a story about harmony and hope. As he began to type he watched the words emerge, but they were not the same as the voice inside his head. It was in that moment that Karl was turned inside out again.

"They write themselves you know," he thought, words and feelings that should be hidden. The story that began writing itself was a story comprised of fragments of emotion that Karl had living inside of himself. Karl had always felt these emotions, but now could not claim them as solely his own. Karl Wright was one of the last of his bloodline, the tip of his family tree; he suddenly realized that his branch of life experience did not grow independently of the rest. The fear, guilt and conflict Karl had experienced his entire life were not his own, they grew within him from the roots from whence he had come. Karl realized that in order for his branch of the family tree to grow and be nourished, purity and peace needed to come from its roots; this meant that Karl would have to undo all of his ancestral pains and hardship from the top down. Karl, however, only had access to one generation below.

Karl realized that in order for him to write his own story of harmony and hope, he had to 'unwrite' his parents' stories of hurt and fear. He wrote about how his father acknowledged that he was not responsible for his own mother's sadness, and that he was a strong and protective man. Karl wrote about how he was never left wanting for money or support and how his dad knew that he was a good father to his children, and a kind and giving husband to his wife. Karl's story explained how his father could feel his own father – a man he never knew – smile upon him with pride at the man that Horst Junior had become.

The words continued to spill onto the computer screen. They told of how Karl's mother had overcome her feelings of loneliness, her protective mask fell away and her kindness was left standing without fear of being perceived as weak. Karl's mom put down her own burdens as well as those that she thought she had to carry for others. Diana was free of all the restrictions that she placed upon herself; contentment and peace flowed over her like summer rain. Karl's story explained how she realized that she was always a pillar of strength to her children and her husband and how she was her father's calm voice of reason and empathy. Diana saw that past hurts have no place in the present – she destroyed them, and she was free.

Karl's story explained how his parents knew that all they set out to achieve in having a family, they did, they were victorious, and Karl's life was testament to that.

Karl sat quietly and stared at the evolution of his thoughts. He wondered what to do with such an unlikely piece. These words were more than just clues hidden in the wind, passing through the leaves and branches of his family tree. They were the beginning of a story, and so he decided to send them to their respective owners. Attached to the email was a note:

"Please read this, digest it and burn it so that the universe may know that we are all not the products of our past, but the architects of our future."

Chapter 3 Friendship

The crew

True friends are the closest things to family in their ability to exhibit unconditional love. I met my closest friends under the strangest of circumstances. The bulk of these kindred spirits arrived in the form of rivals. After my schooling in Natal, I decided to make the move to the city of Cape Town; my then-girlfriend prompted this relocation. She was something from a boyish fantasy. Her large breasts and philosophical outlook made her a good travel partner in our search of a new lifestyle. Moving area codes is a great way to start again with the feeling of limitless potential. But the change was not only foreign, it was sudden too. So with a spanner in my plans and the experience of my first heartbreak, I opened myself up to a variety of new people and new things.

I was studying part-time but it felt as if I was missing out on something. I wrote a letter to the University of Cape Town asking them to give me a chance. They believed in me and I attained my first tertiary qualification from UCT. Fearlessly, with my two new friends, Stuart and Greg, we raced towards the carefree antics of a university student's culture. We were experts at garden football, beer drinking, smooth talking and pushing the limits of our fearlessness. Our egos and newly constructed reputations controlled the everyday decisions we tried desperately to avoid.

We rested upon each other for everything, but we never said anything of the sort. Competitiveness took on a different shape as each of us tried to be the best at rebelling against all types of responsibility. Stuart did this with an ease and charisma that made even the most revered of free spirits jealous and anxious. He had been involved in a NDE (near death experience) a few years before and as a result, had a scar on his face and a new ordering of priorities; friends, family, surfing, girls and mischief. Stuart's most powerful trait was to make anything seem exciting and Greg and I followed enthusiastically.

One Friday night, after a drinking marathon at a nearby nightclub, the three of us had ended up at Stuart's second floor apartment. It was a small bachelor flat, equipped with lava lamps, bean bags and hanging ornaments. One of the two sofas lay against a large framed window that faced the street. When we arrived I screamed "shotgun" and jumped onto the couch as Stuart and Greg walked into the bedroom with devilish intent. Giggles and sneeze like noises slipped through the doorway while shouting and swearing came from the road.

"Someone just shot me with a little fucking pellet gun," declared the male voice.

"Turn the lights off," whispered Stuart as if issuing orders.

I stood up to help the troublemakers, at just about the same time as an empty bottle of beer tore through the glass of the French window and broke on the middle of my back. A chase ensued but the bottle throwers escaped. Injured and insulted, we spent the rest of the night discussing how we were going to find and battle our new adversaries. It was after all, only a plastic bullet.

The variety of creative revenge tactics conjured up over the next few days eventually lost their appeal. The weeks that followed were filled with adventure and the addition of new recruits to the friendship circle. We had met some like-minded guys at university and were enjoying sizing up each other's thirst for adventure and bravery under fire. We tried to outdo another's craziness in order to gain respect. We all succeeded and became inseparable friends. There was an abundance of laughter, concerts, girls, parties and studying.

It was on a usual Wednesday afternoon, during a friendly game of garden cricket that a humorous story about our new friends emerged. One of the guys, Sean, relayed how one night he had been shot by a pellet gun and how he had retaliated by throwing a glass bottle through his attacker's window. Stuart, Greg and I paid close attention for a different reason. We cut Sean short and explained that we were the shooters. They too had set up a revenge strategy after that night but the whole incident had now become both a lesson in life's irony and a great reference point to our actual meeting.

The believed cycle of friendship is that it supposedly fades when you are down and out; friends generally lose contact as their personal demands require more attention than keeping up with those that they held dear. This is the first myth, and it is one that does not hold any truth for me. Our circle expanded, the consequences of our actions seemed greater, and the days and nights got shorter, but when we were called to each other's aid, we answered instantaneously. Sickness and injury are often the catalysts for the expected abandonment. Real friends know how to feel and know how to act in these situations where words and gestures are not strong enough.

The weekend a neurosurgeon discovered the cause of my rapid discomfort, a real friend died in a car accident. Everyone who knew Scottie wept at the news and they relied on each other for lucid memories. He had a questioning mind, a generous heart and a 'take no prisoners' attitude to life. Both coming to terms with our loss and the recovery process were difficult. " Scottie lives in us now," I thought. Phone calls came in by the dozens and the message was clear. "Of all the people this could happen to, we thought you the least likely, but don't worry, we got you buddy," they said with confidence.

My ego defended the rest of my physical status through repeated reassurance as I sat in the hallway of the hospital ward with a saline drip plugged into my left arm. Medical staff are wonderful at making it seem like all is well even when it is not the case. My friends were not trained in the art of consolation via illusion, so their words were aimed at telling me that we would find a way to rectify the damage to my nervous system. They were not aware of the part that they would later play in my recovery.

It was shortly after the hospital visit that one of my prayers was answered, but she is another chapter. Someone once told me that when people interact, there is a transfer of information and energy. Now that we were in our late twenties, the focus on energy allocation and the pursuit of happiness was fast becoming of great importance. But energy can't be destroyed so the myth of death as the final end is exactly that – another myth. My guardian angel (who I'll speak of later) found two controversial treatments once all of the known ones had failed. There was a risk factor attached though and of all things, it was money. Since I had spent all of my resources searching for a cure, the information was useless without the desperately needed energy. She sent an email requesting the help of my kindred spirits and R130 000 ($25 000) was raised and donated within three weeks. An incredible amount to raise in such a short time, but still only two thirds of the way to the required target. The therapies were booked so it was impossible to turn back despite the fact that all available avenues had been explored.

One day I visited my parents and we celebrated the actions of my friends and tried to conjure a plan to raise the rest of the money. My mobile phone rang and on the other end of the line was Scottie's father. We spoke for a while about my plans for stem cell therapy and how fast the departure date was approaching.

"Well, that's why I'm calling," he said. "Scottie had a will drafted before he left us, and one of the stipulations was that a percentage of it was to be given to a friend or charity in need."

I remained silent.

"We want it to go to you and it will be deposited tomorrow," he finished.

The words "thank you" was all I could muster as the tears swelled my eyes. We ended the conversation and three days later the money was deposited in my account, making the total that was needed. Not even death could stop my friend Scottie from loving and helping me.

Meanwhile, the rest of the crew followed up on my developments religiously. The support came in furiously and unwavering – even after my angel and I had returned from Europe. It continues even now and I will introduce them as they reappear. I can describe them with just three words – brothers and sisters.

Chapter 4 Time Travel

You cannot believe the amount of alleged therapies that there are out there, and in my case, I've tried them all. One of the most popular is that of memory regression. It earned a good person's name for its effectiveness in assisting people with cancer. It works if a person can consciously take their mind back to the time of greatest personal suffering and deal with those emotions to try and accept them for what they are. Acceptance became a dirty word and when it was brought up, I thought it meant giving up instead. I chose to bide my time, weather the storm and wait for my hope of salvation to present itself. When life gives you lemons, everyone has the choice to pass on the offer to make lemonade or to find an orange juice vender instead. But while I was waiting, I ran over the past hurts in my life and cleared them away so they could not influence my reactions to neutral events any longer. I needed only to gather the energy that was left behind in a time when I thought authority was held by incompetent older people who ordain themselves as righteous. Patience holds the power of authority, not judgment, and with that in mind, I turned my attention inward and let an unsure confidence find me.

I retraced my steps to the hardest and most confusing period in my life. The clock settled on 1990 when I had rampant hormones and misplaced ambitions. The creative subconscious brewed and another short story flew out of the shadows, bringing with it feelings of rage and disgust. The only thing I could do was let it out and hope it would stay put. The following story is an account of that attempt at time travel.

SHORT STORY

THE QUIET GIRL

Photograph by Claire Young

"Sandra Olivia Smith is a little bitch," blurted one of the teachers from a smoky common room. The teatime gossip was the favorite period of day for all the teachers at St Joan's College. The school was residence to over a thousand teenage girls and had a reputation of grooming the best and most graceful of British model citizens. The careers of politicians, entrepreneurs and artists, not to mention perfect housewives, were forged in its grey walls. But not everyone earned the respect they would acquire later in life during their stay at the prestigious school. Sandra Smith was one of these girls. She was tall and skinny and her green eyes and nervous grin were hidden beneath her red hair.

Sandra's schoolmates and tutors did not like her and they voiced their disapproval at every available opportunity.

"She's too quiet," they would say. Stillness always breeds suspicion in the minds of the unhappy. Sandra never fought back. She stored their cruel words in her heart and she blamed herself for not retaliating. The verbal torments did not stop. "Hey ginger slut," the girls taunted as she passed by. "Why aren't you hiding in the library today?" they would continue. The school library was Sandra's only safe place as talking was forbidden there. It was ironically also the place where Sandra Smith would plot her revenge.

The seventeen-year-old pupils in Sandra's grade were completing their final year at St Joan's College. The days were filled with the scurrying of nervous feet and panic as the year-end approached. The frequency of her classmates ridicule lessened slightly as their attention turned to new activities, but the teachers could not let a soft target go untouched.

Sarcasm is the most violent form of wit and only those who possess it enjoy it. Sandra did not like it and, as such, would later be forced to associate herself with the rebellious and often ostracized, creative crowd. These girls lived to shock. They wore tatty uniforms, dark makeup and seemed to get pleasure from the disapproving gaze that would often follow them. One of these girls was Leanne Brook. She was a short, curvy girl with bleached white hair and a large mouth that could include a profanity in every sentence. This uncontrollable trend often landed her in after-school detention and one afternoon Leanne found herself sitting alongside a defeated and teary redhead.

"What the hell is wrong with you?" asked Leanne with an unsympathetic frown.

"I hate this place," said the demoralized shaking girl.

"We all hate this shitty place, honey, but we are almost free to hate the rest of the world too." The expression on her face had softened as Sandra gasped to speak again.

"I can't leave without letting these people know what it feels like to have their souls destroyed." Silence fell over the room as a teacher entered and Sandra hid her tears once again behind her hair.

"Meet me behind the drama class later," whispered Leanne as the bell rang to signal the end of their punishment.

Sandra walked slowly up to the auditorium. One thing she did like about the school was its aesthetic beauty. The grounds were often covered in an afternoon mist that meandered along the walkways and made the sports fields look like snow-capped mountains. The smell of pine trees was both refreshing and spine chilling. She arrived outside the drama class without having one awkward encounter and as she breathed out a deep sigh of relief, she was startled by the footsteps of Leanne and two other girls. Leanne had a cigarette in her left hand and only raised it to her lips when she was in mid sentence.

"Girls, this is my new friend." Her two companions raised their eyebrows and tightened their lips as if to say hello. "I never got your @#&%ing name," she continued.

"Sandra," she said with an apologetic tone.

"Well Sandra, this is Carla and Debs. We are all part of the special grade."

"What does that mean?"

"It means that our classes are privately tutored and we don't have to do any of the other shit with the other brainwashed idiots." Sandra felt a newfound confidence enter her as she probed deeper.

"How did you end up there?"

"Our parents are extremely wealthy and all the other schools kicked us out – bastards," said one of the other girls matter-of-factly. Sandra couldn't relate. Her parents were not rich but it seemed as though these girls had felt the same embarrassment for different reasons. Carla twirled her brown hair with her fingers and remarked, "Lee says you're after revenge?" Sandra felt her knees start to shake. She knew that these were not the people with whom to lose credibility.

"Hell yes," came the words with a tone she had never heard before.

"Well then you've come to the right place," said Leanne as she put her arm over Sandra's shoulder and escorted her into the building.

The drama assembly building was empty and humid. Plastic green chairs were stacked on either side of the room and the layers of settled dust revealed how infrequently the area was used. The four girls stood facing the stage.

"What do you see?" Leanne asked. The others remained speechless as she kept her eyes fixed on the wooden platform. "I see the last unscrewed part of this school. They should have torn it down when they had the chance."

"But this school doesn't care about plays or drama," exclaimed Sandra.

"They do at the end of year assembly," said Leanne. The back of the hall was a spectacle. It highlighted the hierarchical structure that was forced into each and every student at St. Joan's College. It was the designated seating area for teachers and prefects, which was raised so that it overlooked the stage and entire assembly, resembling a supporter's box at a football stadium. The area was even cased in thick glass to emphasize that all figures of authority ultimately end up displayed in a glass tower, but it actually served to give the teachers free reign to pass judgments and comments during public events. The girls left the empty room, each with a new bounce in their step. As night fell upon the residents of St Joan's, everyone rested safely on the memories of their daily conquests, except for four outcasts that were sitting in a circle on the lawn … conspiring.

The next day came fast and the excitement from the night before was still lingering.

"It felt great," Sandra thought, "to wake up with purpose and not fear."

The anger was, however, still there, causing her to clench her fists all through breakfast. Mornings were frantic at the boarding house. She looked across the tables to find her three new friends staring at her with devilish smiles. Carla waved at her and mouthed the words, "the library," before finishing her meal. Sandra met the girls again at the library that afternoon. She found them huddled up and giggling in the corner cubicle where it was safe to whisper to each other. "Hello," Sandra said under her breath.

"Sit down honey, there's no time for pleasantries," instructed Debbie.

Her role in the cunning plan was simple. She was in charge of getting the materials for surveillance from her boyfriend, who was a boy that prided himself on digitally monitoring strangers and friends. His paranoid antics were exactly what were needed. The wheels of phase one were slowly set in motion. Leanne sat forward and produced a list of names entitled 'Targets'. Sandra added two names to the list as the others nodded in approval. They all salivated when the bell rang that day – thirsty with the thought of what was about to happen. Sandra repeated the list over and over to herself throughout the remainder of that week. The first of the targets was Mrs Bradstrait and the young girl watched her re-affirm her place on the list.

Mrs Bradstrait was a science teacher at the college who enjoyed passing snide remarks during her lessons. It seemed to Sandra that this woman was more interested in destroying her students' confidence than she was in educating them. She would often stand at the front of the class and isolate those learners who reminded her of people that she could not control as a youngster.

"She is a coward who abuses her position," Sandra thought. People who don't learn from their past must hurt again and again, because only fools dare to make the same mistakes twice. Sandra sat at the back of the classroom and fought off the verbal attacks from the silver-haired teacher with a silent contempt. The class ended characteristically with the plump teacher mocking a shy student that could not defend herself adequately. The rest of the students grabbed their books and left before they could become the focus of a tactless joke. Sandra remained seated with her head down and just as Mrs Bradstrait was about to start on her, Carla entered the room.

"One of your tires has gone down, Miss," she said calmly. The woman dropped her black marker on the desk and ran out of the room without speaking to either of the girls.

"We only have a second," Carla mumbled as he pulled out a handful of black wires and small round gadgets that looked like watch batteries.

"Are you sure she won't find them?" Sandra asked while Carla burrowed through the teacher's handbag.

"She's more likely to find them in your bag," exclaimed Carla with one raised eyebrow. Three of the devices were delicately planted before the two girls made their way to the library.

"What's the rush, ginger slut?" laughed Victoria. She was both the head girl and the most complimented girl at St. Joan's – Miss Popular. Why she did not like Sandra was a mystery.

"Cat got your tongue?" she came again with feet pointing slightly outwards and her shoulders tightly pinned back. The worst thing about Victoria was her entourage. Snarling dogs that repeated everything Victoria said, followed by what sounded like canned laughter.

Carla clumsily bumped into Victoria, saving Sandra. "Oops," said Carla as the two of them entered the library. The screams and echoes became fainter as the girls made their way further down the library passageway towards Debs and Leanne.

"We did it!!" said Sandra proudly, "We bugged the Dragon."

"Not only her," added Carla, "we got Victoria Beckett too."

"How did you get a transmitter on that skank?" asked Leanne out the side of her mouth.

"We bumped into her outside," proclaimed Carla with a smirk. A gleam came across Leanne's face as she started to cross the names off her list.

The next on the hit list was Mr Prince, a personal adversary of Debbie's. He had been responsible for Debbie's periodic stutter that only occurred when he confronted her in his Geography class.

The girls stayed late at the library to test their very new and very complicated audio receiver device. They followed, to the last letter, the implicit instructions that had come with their new device and before they knew it, the girls heard Mrs Bradstrait's patronizing voice on the telephone. They listened tentatively to two women speaking about, what seemed to be, archaic omens and rituals. Leanne pressed the record button and hid the oval-shaped box behind a bookshelf. The girls then departed to have dinner at their respective hostels.

Sandra did not sleep well that night; the reality of what she had done had unhinged her. She tossed and turned but could not find a position that would erase the image of the teachers discovering her treachery. At 5:00 am, her feelings of concern became anger and finally a calm numbness that steadied her into unconsciousness. The worst part of a sleepless night is the day that follows. Sandra spent the morning in the school chapel where Reverend Chase delivered his particularly long-winded weekly sermon. He spoke extensively about the different tools of the devil and that they were ever present – even at schools.

"No shit," thought Sandra. She started to understand, with a sleep-deprived clarity, how powerful the use of fear could be. It could even turn people to God if they feared the presence of evil enough. She suddenly did not feel like her anxiousness was exclusively her own to bear.

"We must fight our human urges and repent before Satan takes hold of our souls," the priest finally concluded. As soon as the students were let out of the poorly lit chapel, every word Reverend Chase had said was forgotten. They were grateful to be free of the tall, balding man's lectures. As they queued outside, Carla shouted to Debbie,

"You're up, Debs."

Debbie sat at the front of the classroom during her Geography lesson. Mr Prince knew all too well how to use the command of fear in his daily classes. He sporadically shouted out his words, which made his students jolt in their seats – an effective tool to ensure everyone's constant attention. He waved his cane around like a knight's sword as he conquered his first period students. Mr Prince always wore old clothes and beneath his thick beard was an old face. He was never seen without his beige suede jacket though, and this was exactly what Debbie spent the lesson staring at with a purposeful gaze. Her moment came when he asked someone to fetch his glasses from his jacket pocket.

"I'll get it, sir?" she asked.

"Well hurry up then, girl!" As Debbie took his glasses from the jacket pocket, she slipped a tiny microphone into the pocket. He did not thank her for fetching his glasses, but rather took the opportunity to confront her at the chalkboard. She began to stutter again until she was ordered to "Sit down, bloody girl!"

The small black machine lay patiently underneath the corner bookshelf, recording the conversations and daily activities if Mr Prince, Mrs Bradstrait and Victoria Becket. Meanwhile, the girls met every afternoon to have what they called 'status meetings'. Over three weeks had passed and the girls had monitored no additional targets. The girls' initial thrill was growing thin but they had become close friends and when friends lose enthusiasm, they dig deep.

Leanne stormed into the library holding a blue, bowl-shaped ornament.

"What is that ugly thing?" asked Carla.

"It's an ashtray," she replied. Leanne could see from their animated frowns that were puzzled. She sighed and lifted the bowl to her face.

"I made it in art class and I don't think I'll be allowed to keep it at this school." The others gazed at her with confused, blank expressions.

"Then why did you make it?" enquired Sandra.

"Wait and see," she said. "Just make sure that bug seven is active on the machine." Debbie did as requested and Leanne left, still holding the ominous creation above her shoulders.

In Biology class Leanne put her work of art at the edge of her desk. It took twenty-three-and-a-half minutes before it was confiscated. As he took it, Mr Giffin said, "You won't be needing this until the end of the year, missy." Leanne thought to herself, "You take it, asshole."

When class was over, Mr Giffin proudly carried his trophy to the teachers' common room. He was pleased with his new find and he grinned uncontrollably at the door. Mr Giffin was an avid gossiper and conspiracy theorist, the teachers all laughed as he walked them through the story of how he acquired their new and custom-made teatime ashtray. He embellished a bit on the details of his morning encounter and even the Reverend found the whole ordeal quite entertaining.

Mr Kraft picked up the ceramic bowl, which was now the focus of attention. He was, after all, the headmaster of the school, and he scrutinized its every imperfection.

"I wouldn't buy it," he said with a disapproving sneer. He turned it over to find Leanne's initials painted on the base next to a small red and black ladybug, he snarled, and banged it onto the centre of the common room table before leaving to attend to more important school matters. The teachers immediately put the ashtray to use.

"It was very kind of Leanne to donate this to us," said Mrs Bradstrait, not realizing the significance of the sweet and harmless ladybug that lay at the bottom of their new accessory. While the teachers gossiped, the four girls triumphantly listened from a musky library cubicle.

Two days had passed since Leanne had infiltrated the enemy's lair. Mr Kraft addressed the school as usual on Friday morning's assembly; he stood at the podium like a dictator.

"I would first like to congratulate the final-year students on a successful academic year, and would like to remind them that there are only two months left until graduation. It is imperative that you all remain focused, the reputation of the school's past achievements lies on your shoulders, and the staff and I will be watching you all closely. Girls, the world out there is predatorial, so don't leave anything to chance." He pointed his finger towards the sea of anxious faces. "Furthermore, this institution does not accept failure, but the teachers and I are all, as usual, looking forward to the annual year-end drama performances." Sandra and her three comrades were all thinking the same thing, "You may be the eyes, but we are the ears of this school."

Sometimes the hunters become the hunted. The pupils were all shaken up after the assembly; they scribbled tight schedules into their diaries, planning every moment of the two months that lay ahead. Victoria Beckett had another solution; when academic pressure became too much, she outsourced the talents of Rebecca Stuart, who frequently supplied her with lecture and study notes. She repaid Rebecca with empty promises of popularity and social fame. Rebecca believed her lies every time and after five years of manipulation, had resigned herself to the fact that she could avoid further social turbulence by simply doing what was asked of her. Victoria rolled her eyes after another one of these plastic encounters and all the students at St Joan's slowly gravitated towards their respective lessons.

"Oh Rebecca," cried Victoria before the timid girl could escape, "don't forget I need your help for the drama script." What she really meant was, "I want you to write the end of year script so I can take the credit for your hard work, one last time!" The head girl even had a name for her different types of persuasion. This one was called 'the snowball'. She put on a sympathetic expression, which Rebecca returned with a look of demoralized understanding.

The four girls stood together and re-arranged their schedules in a different way. They scheduled a status meeting during lunch that day, to discuss the audio recordings that were building in the library. Leanne took control of the meeting.

"Ok, there are eight channels and four of us, so each person is responsible for gathering information from their two channels." There were no objections and they drew up a roster to split the workload. The work was, however, time-consuming and tedious. It was amazing how much babbling and fruitless conversation took place behind closed doors. "Guess what?" said Carla on the Sunday evening.

"I've been listening to Mr Prince, it turns out, he has been having an affair with one of the other teachers at this school!" The others sat with tilted heads.

"Who?" they asked eagerly, while pondering the implications and repercussions of such information on Mrs Prince.

"Our very own – Mr Giffin," she giggled. The girls sat crossed-legged and shocked. "'You are @#&%ing kidding?" cried Leanne. "Every night they meet to educate each other." Misery always seeks its mirror image. The girls laughed at the discovery they had made and later in the hostel they joked about it for hours. Those two men were the names that Sandra had added to the original list and that night she slept so deeply that not even the screams of excitement in the other dormitories could disturb her.

Two weeks had passed and the girls began to doubt whether any new secrets were going to be found. Sandra had grown tired of Victoria's boastful antics and the teacher's common room seemed only to reveal fabricated classroom stories. Between the third and fourth period Debbie found Sandra standing at the bottom of a cold staircase. She had listened in on a very interesting conversation between Victoria and her pack of wild dogs. She did not pause once as she told Sandra the truth about the elected spokesperson for the student council. It turned out that Victoria's extracurricular activities included sneaking boys from the neighboring college into the boarding house after sunset. She was also underhandedly giving naked pictures of her friends to Reverend Chase in return for his cooperation.

"That explains all the noises at night," added Sandra. The girls were tempted to disclose these secrets when they came under fire from the relevant offenders, but it was not the time to bite back. The evidence was labeled and stored, not to be addressed until every person on the list had been trapped by his or her own misdeeds.

Mrs Bradstrait lived in a stone cottage at the front entrance of the school. She had two black cats that she spoke to constantly. The exterior of the cobblestone house was a mirage. As a form of initiation and at least once during the year, the first year students would sneak up to the house and steal one of the cacti on the windowsill. The inside of the vine-covered structure was filled with old furniture and decorated with an array of colorful, scented candles. Units 1 and 2 were recording the activities of the bitter and private Mrs Bradstrait. The monitors however, had not listened in on these channels for nearly a week and had missed the unveiling of her true nature. Huddled up in the corner once again, the four girls reviewed the weeklong recording. A shriek came over the headphones, followed by a language that sounded like Latin.

"So bode it," was the final part of her raging. Debbie looked at her team members with wide eyes.

"I know what she's doing. She's casting a spell." The girls returned to those first two channels religiously and discovered that not only was Mrs Bradstrait casting spells, but curses too.

"I always knew she was a witch," sighed Sandra.

Only five weeks remained in the school year. The exams were over and it was time for the students to rejoice in the celebration of having completed a pinnacle stage in their lives. The four girls were only on the second stage of their plans. The traps had been set, and the next stop was Rebecca.

They approached her with a definitive proposal, which she agreed to, even before they had finished pitching. That afternoon, Rebecca approached Victoria for the first time.

"The script is almost ready," she said.

"Just make me one of the heroes," replied Victoria with a superior voice. It was the first time Rebecca had lied to her pushy adversary; the four girls had taken over the responsibility of writing the script for the year-end production. The play was a tradition at St Joan's. Each year, it was (allegedly) written by the head girl and performed by the first years as a symbolic handing over of the school torch. The teachers enjoyed the shows as they poked fun at the unpopular girls and reinforced the authoritative roles of the tutors and prefects.

The girls worked very hard at the script, while the other ignorant students spent their last few days at the school sun bathing on the hockey fields. Victoria Beckett and company came up with nicknames for all the unpopular girls at the school. Sandra and her new friends were referred to as the 'freaky four', but that did not deter them from finishing the script.

Their plan was almost flawed by Mrs Greene. She was a slow speaking, kind teacher who taught Sandra graduate English. During her second-last lesson, Mrs Greene came across Sandra hastily writing a section of the script – not paying attention to her final words of wisdom.

"What you doing there, Miss Smith?" she questioned.

"Nothing ma'am," Sandra responded. She removed the pages from Sandra's desk and put them on her briefcase, continuing the lesson.

"Do you think she'll read it?" asked Carla when Sandra told them the news. It was too late to turn back and the script writing was once again confined to the library. The storyline was completed the day before the performance. Leanne leant over and switched the recorder on. It was time to listen in on channel seven for one last time. The usual common room jokes did not come up. Instead, there was only the sound of Mr Kraft on the telephone. He was performing his yearly ritual of secluded cigar smoking in his office and having an intense conversation about school finances.

"He must have borrowed the common room ashtray," Leanne thought. She put down the earpiece and moved closer to the other girls.

"We are not finished yet," she said taking a sip of her water. The girls listened over and over to the discussion between Mr Kraft and his financial adviser. The last minute editing of Leanne's swear words to the pages and some other modifications were made to the screenplay.

"One day until show time," said Sandra.

The next morning at 11:00 am, the students of St Joan's College spilt into the assembly hall for the show. Sandra and her friends took their places on the green chairs while the teachers and prefects made their way up the small staircase to the gala viewing area above. It was as much a performance for the teachers as it was for the students and parents. They acted as if they had never met each other when the schoolgirl's parents twisted their heads to look up at them. The audience settled once the teachers had finished pretending. Sandra felt her heart pounding in her chest when Victoria got to her feet and moved towards the podium.

"Bravery," thought Sandra, "is felt in the stomach."

Victoria had only received the script ten minutes earlier from Rebecca. It was customary for the young, eighth grade actors not to receive their lines until the actual performance. Half the fun was usually had by watching them fumble through their pages on stage. The writer, however, normally spent the night before reading the script, not preparing her opening speech.

Victoria cleared her throat into the microphone.

"Good morning fellow schoolmates, teachers and guests. It is with great pride that I get to open today's proceedings. I have learnt many things about myself, and this institution, over my past five years at this school. The teachers have been a great source of inspiration to me, my friends and many other girls here today. I only hope that this performance does justice to the many different things that you do at St Joan's. Please excuse me if this year's play is a bit conservative but I wanted it to be as realistic and true as possible. I hope that it is as enjoyable for you to watch, as it was for me to write. It is without further ado that I present to you, 'Ode to St Joan's.'"

Victoria made her way down the aisle and up the staircase to sit with the teachers. Everyone clapped except for the teachers, who saved their approval for when she had reached them. They congratulated her, safe in their soundproof box. Leanne had positioned herself at the back of the hall and once Victoria had entered through the staircase door, placed a rusted broom across the handles, locking the teachers in. The young and inexperienced actors had an eager, or rather, captive audience. Everyone shifted slightly as the curtain lifted. An atmosphere was set by the vibrations of Radiohead.

The entire production was set in the teachers' common room and lasted just over thirty minutes. The audience was extremely receptive and they hung onto every word spoken, breaking their attention only to swivel their chairs and see the teacher's reactions. The teachers took a few minutes to realize that they were viewing their extinction like lobsters watching a restaurant crowd through a glass tank.

"Ain't art a bitch," thought Carla.

Mr Prince hid at the feet of Mr Giffin, who was clenching his fists frantically. Mr Kraft banged on the glass screaming and frothing at the mouth while Mrs Bradstrait just sat and marveled at the sheer genius of the deception. All the usual mannerisms of the teachers were illustrated, but this year, had a substantially more revealing storyline. It was a wonderful performance that portrayed a teacher as a witch, a homosexual relationship between two others, a church member with a fetish for young girls, a schoolgirl with compromised morals and a headmaster who was embezzling school money.

The grade eight parents grabbed at their mobile phones when they left the assembly hall, all of them acquiring the services and advice of their lawyers. The teachers and prefects clawed with anguish and horror at the glass walls but they had no role to play in the *coup d'etat*. It took another thirty minutes before they were released, ranting and raving from their glass tower. Their rescuers were wearing black and white uniforms. The police were also in possession of some interesting audiotapes that were found underneath Victoria Becket's bed. The parents stood in small groups and looked on as the guilty teachers were dressed in new, silver handcuffs. Sandra smiled at Victoria and the teachers when they were escorted to the flashing cars. Victoria made eye contact with Sandra and started to scream and proclaim her innocence.

"It wasn't me; it was Sandra Smith and her freaky friends."

"Don't you dare try and blame it on the quiet girl," instructed the captain of police with a stern voice.

The last day of school was unusually still. Red tape surrounded most of the classrooms, the boarding house, the school chapel, the admin block and even Mrs Bradstrait's house. There was a significant shortage of teachers and graduates that day when Sandra went to get her yearbook signed by Mrs Greene. When she reached the front of the line, the gentle woman greeted her.

"So you're leaving us today?" she said.

"Yes, Ma'am. Will you sign my book?" Mrs Greene gave the magazine back to Sandra but as the girl was leaving, she called to her.

"Miss Smith, I never gave this back to you." Mrs Greene was holding the confiscated pages of the screenplay.

"Did you read it," asked the redheaded girl nervously.

"Yes, but I didn't want to ruin the actual debut performance."

"Thank you, Mrs Greene," Sandra took back the pages and stared admiringly at the teacher for what felt like hours.

The corridors did not feel cold to Sandra that day. She tied her hair into a ponytail and stepped into her dad's car. They drove through the golden gates of the school for the last time.

Sandra gazed out the passenger window at the plain trees and thought about the weeks that had passed. Her right hand was tucked safely behind her father's neck.

"You should wear your hair back more often," said her father, "and let everyone see what you are made of."

"I think they know now," she replied.

Silence followed and Sandra closed her eyes.

A smile came over her face and she sighed deeply.

THE END

I didn't find any closure after the story was done. It made me relive the experience of feeling wounded all over again. The process of trying to overcome those emotions was easier said than done. Meditation and affirmations seemed to only transform denial into sadness. The underlying message of memory regression is to learn the technique of acceptance. This is what most people believe. We all need to go through hard times in order to appreciate the good times as happy rather than mundane. That, and the ideology that it's all a test of strength and character. This is what I believe I learnt. We need to learn things the hard way and formulate a definite idea about ourselves and others, only so we can later disprove those theories to find one of the only constant truths. Life is played out by an interesting uncertainty. The walk down memories' dark lane made me think about authority, who I used to think had it and who ultimately decides on whether a person deserves it.

"It all depends on judgment," I thought.

Well in that case, sorry Einstein, but there is no such thing as time travel. There is, however, a perfect time for nearly everything. Carl Jung called the precise ordering of all events, 'synchronicity'. It is the fundamental cornerstone to how we live forwards and understand backwards and while such a theory is useful during dinner conversation; the problem is one of practical application. The test subjects are usually desperate as I have been, so control over one's fate is often left with the burnt-out candles at the end of the night. I meditated and prayed, trying with every morsel of energy to summon a cure from nothingness.

Chapter 5 Faith

It is possible, through the use of hindsight, to make sense of chaos. I have subscribed and believed in many things since the bomb first dropped two years ago. The easiest thing to buy into was the words and logic of others. They seemed, not only fathomable, but also gave them a sense of purpose and meaning, which I desperately craved. I didn't realize then that their passionate claims were mostly voiced to convince themselves time and time again. There was an undeniable thread and common trait that ran through each encounter, though, and it was that of calm. Remaining still is an art that everyone tries to master. It is obvious to me that all of life's answers reside in that space, and once I knew that truth, I visited it religiously every night before bed. These insights spilt over into the days until logic and mysticism became my normal mode of existing and searching, but the two could not coexist. I sat on the fence for many months and pondered the most effective coping technique from the fashionable.

The allure of past and specifically ancient remedies was great. I wasn't trying to reinvent the wheel but I did want to use it to get to my destination with ease. So I poured over books, listened to compact discs that were filled with ancient wisdom and associated myself with the likes of deep and troubled souls. Affirmations are frequently employed to eradicate health problems by these techniques, and I learnt them all. Exotic phrases passed my lips like I had known them since birth but no amount of Latin or Sanskrit sentences could penetrate my doubts, despite their consuming appeal. I tested their impact on my physical obstacles daily and, whilst consoling, they left me wanting for more. So the only thing was to discover my own affirmations in my own language that were tailor-made to my desires. Spasticity plagued my every movement and prevented me from reaching smoothly for things and stretching outwards without encountering a violent epileptic-type state. Before I attempted such a feat, I would repeat the words "I will not fear that which I have overcome already!" This simple declaration calmed my nerves instantly and stilled my anxiety for the movements that were needed. They were my answer to fear and uncertainty.

After I returned from Holland, I began to crash even though my optimism was high. I scheduled physiotherapy for every day of the week and I threw my body at each exercise with words of amazement. The therapist was a middle-aged woman who seemed more concerned with proving her own qualifications than increasing mine. I was running out of power faster than the placebo thoughts could keep up with. I phoned my family each day and embellished on the details of what was happening. Total honesty was exclusively reserved for times of prayer when I could emotionally afford to surrender. It was like opening my eyes to the calm understanding that it was alright for things to be out of my hands for then and I slept peacefully each night on that belief. Believing and knowing are entirely two different things and it took years to tell the two apart. My prayers became monotonous and I changed only the context. The known answers to these pleas appeared comforting and helpful. They gave me the sensation that all was under control from the other side. I just wanted to see them materialize before my troubles were all I knew.

I concluded that the climate in Johannesburg was not conducive to healing as the cells should have taken more of an effect at that time. Nona and I discussed the options of relocating somewhere new and in November 2005 we moved to Cape Town where the residents endorse creativity and potential. It was a constructive attempt at running from the storm and for a while it worked. I woke each morning with tears of joy at the sight of an awesome mountain and the sounds of birds chirping. My younger sister, Cheri, whom I had not lived near for over ten years, was also staying in Cape Town. It was good, regardless of the reasons for being there. Whenever I heard people saying I should go to a quiet, safe place, I always thought of that city.

Sanctuaries are present, even when tragedy comes calling and the last thing left to do, was get the Big Guy involved in my recovery process. Faith, it seems, was carried out by being thankful for the things you have not received yet. The prayers continued through the times of doubt, over a thousand tears and beyond all hope. I came to the conclusion that I must be doing it wrong. Aside from the feelings that God was there, I felt totally abandoned. I tried to keep my chin up by attributing lessons to every symptom suffered, thereby trying to let the same brain that caused the problem find a way out of that tunnel. I had moved from my knees to beneath the floorboards. But faith doesn't need reasoning. I see that now. It is like trying to know the source by analyzing its products.

I still attempted to let my brain drive and chose the reasons behind my rapid demise. My body had adapted and mutated, adjusting to the weekly changes. One of the expected changes felt like a ton of bricks. It was the decrease in eyesight ability and with it came a skewed but logical rationale. I took it as a clue, salted proof that life was telling me: "Just because you can't see something, it doesn't mean that it's not there." I prayed and meditated even harder to learn from the opportunity to connect with the ever-present conductor. The left side of my body went limp and lame so I decided it was also an indication of how to modify my thinking. I interpreted it to mean that I should not try to hold on so tight to things. This new approach to hardship offered little relief. While my mind made sense of the problems, my soul knew the deal, which a simple brain could never comprehend.

The workings of prayer are even more difficult to wrap ones head around. Its non-negotiability dictates that all prayers are answered but not at the convenience of the person asking. This is to say, that a series of events must be re-ordered before the request can be carried out. My obvious reaction to this was to be careful what I wished for but the rabbit hole extends further than caution, and although desires change, the soul is still in the driving seat. I always asked for things bigger than I could imagine. Mediocrity was my greatest fear and it is no surprise that the road has been riddled with so many bumps and turns of fortune.

"Please make me a healer of pain, larger than life, the centre of epiphanies and make my path greater than those who have walked before me."

I think back now and wonder what I thought would happen when those words fell on the right ears. The name itself should be changed from 'faith' to 'trust' and that definitely requires patience to be exercised along the way. Aloof people like my blessed sister Cheri, think that they emanate a personality that is relaxed and humble. It is a choice for her not to acknowledge that she wrestles less with intent than she does with incentive. I know because I was once one of those people, screaming from the inside and pushing my own nature aside. People filled in the gaps. They saw me as shy, disinterested, even though I felt that I had done nothing wrong to be made to feel so weak or even, boring. I did feel numbed by my own avoidance tactics. Something was needed to help me break away from my sedated character. At the tender age of sixteen, I reached out for the unconditional promise of peace and resolution. This was the first occasion that I came across a universal truth that goes against everything taught to us by others. It is quite simply that we don't know anything in the big scheme of things. I know very little about myself and even less about others. Not only that, but I know nothing about life or what purpose it serves, let alone how to control its movements. The impact this had on my faith was strong. Faith is now not a difficult choice that I make or struggle to uphold. It is the only option I have to stop the pointless fighting and frustration from defining me.

Chapter 6 Authority

When I became physically compromised, desperation and panic drove the frantic attempts to seek out things that promote extreme recovery. At that stage, my mobility was running at 50% and each step was becoming more difficult to place, as my legs were replaced by lead pipes. The reason why medical doctors prescribe the weakest medication first, is so there are other options if it doesn't work. I unwittingly followed this reasoning and booked an appointment with a practicing homeopath. She was an elderly woman, dressed in a white uniform, with a brown jersey and a gold necklace. Her name was Dr Heplim but her assistant just called her Doctor. She walked with a limp that revealed the years she had been practicing natural medicine. She did not command authority or offer much reassurance. I was left with a feeling of wavering hope and a shoebox of tablets and tonics after our consultations. The manner in which she spoke was both slow and sympathetic. She looked like a great candidate for making fresh tea and biscuits, while listening to the concerns of others. Sometimes, a person who listens is all that is needed to dissolve someone's personal anguish. In the physical realm, however, more than sympathy is required.

"She's really good you know, she prescribes a lot of pills, but she's really good," said the secretary from her elevated stool. I was on strict regimen of close on 100 tablets per day, they each had a purpose and when the doctor told me of them, they made perfect sense, but all I did know about the naturalist approach was smoking grass and hiking outdoors. The doctor's scripts did not have the benefit of either of these activities. Her sympathy and multitude of pills seemed like they were standing idly by and waiting for a placebo effect to arrive. While watching my bank balance dissipate, the sweet, understanding, old doctor and I parted ways as my strength deteriorated, despite her good intentions and efforts.

The next appointment was with my allocated neurologist, Dr Cohen. After my doctor had examined me thoroughly, I popped the big question and put him under the limelight.

"Am I ever going to be normal again, Doc?" I asked.

"Probably not," he answered in a monotone voice.

It was cruel of me to put him on the spot while he was wearing his game face. The thing he didn't realize was that I have never been normal and my mode of survival had shifted to one of sheer stubbornness and tenacity. He then began to start listing the other available chemical options I could investigate. He was a youngish and, no doubt, good physician who had seen too many young and good people waste away. He too, did not offer any guarantee that I would come out of this fight triumphant. He was, however, empathetic to my dilemma. He identified the problem and he felt sorry for me for what I was about to endure. Empathy must have been next on the evolutionary scale after sympathy, but still did not have the ability to offer a viable solution for me.

So I was on my own again.

"If the answer wasn't in the natural reordering of things, then it must lie in the spiritual realm. I surrounded myself with books and the well-acknowledged teachings of spiritual healers. They all spoke of love but my question was always the same in response to these assertive confessions:

"How do you love something that you can't see, touch, taste, smell or hear?"

Nevertheless, I began to pray to the illusive concept; after all I did not find the answer in my own history or in my current teachers.

My heart began to pound once I had made contact with the first of many self-proclaimed spiritual healers and teachers. Their individual belief systems are not important. I was the lab rat for their claims of owning healing properties. Most of these accepting healers were unknowing slaves to the allure of dispensing judgment upon their patients through logic alone. Karma, original sin and all the other guidelines are not set by man. I think the best we can do is follow them with faith in our minds and love in our hearts. The result is an uncontrollable kindness and compassion that emanates through our words and actions. I don't want to preach because I don't have the authority to force my beliefs on anyone and god forbid, pass judgment on anyone, although it is my story, so once again, here goes.

Mathematical or clinical equations have never been my forte, but it is obvious to me that some are no-brainers if you look at them honestly.

Compassion = empathy + intention + love + action

No wonder it's so hard. I don't think I'll get a Nobel Prize for my deduction, but maybe you'll get the point. If you do, then you already know which of these variables is the hardest to find – love. At only twenty-eight years old, it is the marinade of my will. It's sweet and consoling, nourishing and delicious.

Chapter 7 The Ideal

I used to think love was an addictive choice that was made. Some people take pills, some throw themselves off bridges and some seek refuge in the instant gratification of food. I prided myself on the conquests of women. Too much Hollywood viewing made me feel like I was reinforcing myself as a champion of collecting hearts and at the end of each encounter, was a disappointing realization that I wasn't the lead in a feature film. So I looked at my addiction and was faced with the understanding that all the girls in the world could not feed my insatiable hunger for perfection. None of them could fill the void that I had created by trying to mould them into the women that could make me drop my guard for them to see inside because I thought they might be let down by what they found. One had come close, but we started growing apart as soon as it felt cemented by words repeated over and over. We did not outgrow each other, but rather, outgrew the excitement of that era when we thought ourselves young enough to know it all.

Johannesburg has a similar allure as any dependant substance. It is the one of the largest human-made urban jungles and in it are the promises of wealth and the route to a competent and mature adulthood. It was for me, a hopeful place to prove myself justified in my own arrogance. I was seeing a pretty girl called Kerry-Ann. She was beautiful and I got lost in her eyes. I hid the terrible news of my first diagnosis from her. She was too young and I had to protect her. We are now friends and she keeps me in supply of really good music. I still miss that beautiful girl. Ruffled sheets and folded paper are not evidence of any value system; they are signs of selfish intentions, the easily identifiable signs of loneliness.

I moved to Johannesburg anyway, searching for acknowledgement and a renewal of faith in the idea of ideal love. What I did not know was that my ideals would not prepare me for my pre-destined encounter with what poets and musicians have tried their entire lives to define. European living and trips to exotic islands were not powerful CV attributes, but who would have thought? My profession had changed from being a self-assured professional model, to running a character agency that specialized in placing people in television advertisements. The lure and bait used was that of an empty promise and part ownership from a guy who was a sexually insecure jester who thought himself king. The calmest moment I had during that period was when I saw an electric fan blowing a plastic packet. I saw the connectedness of everything.

Despite knowing all of that, I worked six days a week trying to build a cardboard kingdom when she walked into my office with a sweet demeanor and shiny cheeks. I couldn't help feel like I had known her from somewhere before. She positioned herself next to me at the computer and as we spoke, I could see that she was intimidated by the décor of cameras and her new surroundings. We chatted gently and had no idea how deeply we would rely on each other or how much those three overused words would be tested over the next two years. I tried everything humanly possible not to give my heart to her, but she was determined to be by my side from that moment on, and now there is no amount of words or displayed affection that could ever show her what she really is to me. After going through suspicion, anger, tears, tenderness and my physical demise together, we decided that something more powerful than us was at work. Her name was Nona and she had given herself that title as soon as she had learnt to speak. Nona was a living myth, headstrong and lovely at a glance. Her strength of character and argumentative conviction pushed a lot of people away but she was in training for the big game with the highest of stakes. Up until then I thought I had it all worked out: different women for different needs. Thank goodness I abandoned my search for happiness on that road but not before trying to intellectualize the unexplainable. I was definitely not the first person in the world to attempt this.

Over the next two years, the twenty-two-year-old girl was present through a hell that is unknown to most mature women. For this I am eternally grateful. She held my hand in countless hospitals, wet my body at four in the morning through fiery temperatures, whispered consoling words when I was in so much pain that I wanted to die and she implemented plans for my recovery that even doctors said were unrealistic. The little redhead makes everyone paying attention to her want to drink chocolate, eat meat from the bone and look forward to the next time they can spend a few minutes in her presence. That's what I thought, anyway. The romantic in me stirred again. She had carried me up narrow staircases and lowered me into the bathtub on too many occasions. The physical obstacles were accompanied by traumatic accidents and on a late Thursday evening trip to the bathroom, my stomach gave way and I was covered in waste. I turned my jittery head in her general direction and asked: "How can you do this when I am so filthy and broken?"

"Because I love you baby, I see you for who you are and there's no space left for any of this stuff," is all she said as I sunk deeper into the water.

I can relay our relationship only by starting from the beginning. This is her story as I saw her and how we became what we were. It is one of the most accurate accounts of that which cannot be explained.

SHORT STORY

The Angel

Painting by Wendy Knights>>

There are no queues in heaven. There is no time, no space and no noise. Souls are separated by their accumulated knowledge and the earth is their playground. No description of this place has ever done justice to the beauty and serenity that exists there. The human explanation for the afterlife is a blissful emotion and the best description for the before-life is a waiting room without the drive to get processed quickly. There are no concrete forms or paperwork, just the desire to have a human experience. Thought is all that is required to travel as the souls prepared to sign their contracts and their life paths. Most of the sentient beings choose the shape of diamonds to represent themselves in the room. Perhaps this is because they reflect the light and love which brought them to the decision of pursuing another series of feelings. The coordinators and the source of these entities are always happy to comply with their wishes.

The ability to choose is the greatest freedom in the universe and the availability of options insures that it does not go to waste. The diamonds had all known each other from past earthly encounters and they willfully chose to re-make the ways in which they would meet again. Two souls, in particular, had spent over 3 000 years finding each other. They were in the waiting room for the last time. When they were asked to plot their lives, they were both unsure about the details. They had been siblings, enemies, friends and relatives.

"In this life we want to be lovers again," requested one of the travelers. Structure exists even in heaven and a covenant must approve all life choices before they are embarked upon. The judicious navigators looked like three large blue crystals as they reviewed the plans. The appeal, however, was seemingly impossible.

"One of you is set to become an angel," they said in unison. The couple had never been through a life without each other. "Only one of you can go through the cycle but the other must simply be a guide and observer," they concluded. The travelers agreed to the terms and conditions of the counsel. The second soul chose a life of relative hardship in order to fully know the pleasure and pain of human existence and being a man. He had always chosen to be a masculine figure in his past lives and the last run would be no different. His soul mate was more intrinsically feminine and she had therefore found it easier to perform acts of self-sacrifice. These selfless moments had promoted her to the title of angel. "See you in a second," she said as her partner passed through the gates into mortality.

The soul landed as a screaming mass of wet flesh. All of his past memories had been erased and an overwhelming need for survival had taken over. He was given the name 'Carlos' by his human guardians in Santorini, and, wrapped in a towel, was taken to his new household. It was a wonderful and new experience for the young creation. Everything appeared colorful and full of substance. He had been born in the country of Greece – the land of olive oil and hedonism. His parents were very kind but very poor by common standards. His induction into the land of the living was not an easy one. By the age of eleven, Carlos had learnt to speak English by listening to the melodies of Collective Soul. He helped his father to transport tourists between the sun-filled islands.

Later, Carlos sought comfort in the arms of women. He looked for something he had once known, but now, could not find. His body was sculptured like the statues that surrounded the island. He grew into his bone structure and facial features by the time he hit his early twenties. The consistent interest he got from girls caused his mother many sleepless nights and much concern. Carlos had long, soft brown hair, chiseled cheekbones and bright green eyes. Tourists would often comment on how they looked like emeralds in the daylight. He had become the pride and accepted trophy of the island. His reputation had extended across watery channels and eventually over continents as the great Greek lover. It was a world of dreams for the young boatman. When he was twenty-one, a talent scout spotted Carlos walking on the harbor's cliff face. She had watched him move along the water's edge until they finally met.

"I'm Penny Lane," she introduced herself with an extended arm.

"Carlos," he replied apologetically. She was momentarily in awe of his calm demeanor and antiquity.

"I'm glad this happened," she assured him. Her accent was hard to place. She was undoubtedly European and well put together. "Enticing," thought Carlos as she spoke.

"I represent a model agency in Milan and I would love to show you to my colleagues at the office." Carlos only recognized the word love as the woman in a white bikini spoke and he was flashed by an image of a majestic girl standing before him with sunflowers in her eyes. He agreed to have dinner with her that evening and discuss it further. Penny was incredibly organized and flattering that night. She told him all the ways in which she was going to make him famous. He walked her back to her hotel that night but declined her offer to have a nightcap. She found him at the docks each day. He enjoyed the attention but could not remove the picture of sunflowers from his mind. Sometimes people get tempted by the way others make them feel about themselves, rather than the way they feel about those people.

Carlos asked her not to return the following day. She left quietly and a bit fascinated by his words of rejection. As he watched her walk off the beach, he felt a gentle embrace around his chest and a soft breath of wind on his neck. Startled, he turned around to find no one within a hundred yards of the motorboat. The water was transparent in the twilight that day. Carlos delivered his final load of tourists. He put the small boat into full throttle and he enjoyed the liberation of his thoughts. It had been a profitable day for tourism on the Greek island. The skipper replayed the day's activities in his head; while he watched the scattered blue and white houses get closer. He wondered why he had not responded to the advances of any of the female holiday-makers that month. The boat did not glide across the mirrored ocean that day. A noise that emanated from the hull eventually began to buzz in the ears of the driver. He moved to the front and saw the frame. Danger does not announce itself. The boat lifted over the swells, forcing Carlos to dance with the new momentum. He respected the power of the sea but over-confidence creates its own surprises. He stood on the deck and compensated for the rocking motion of the graphite boat. A twisted wave moved under the vessel, causing the young man to stumble and fall onto a folded rope by the storage box. His head turned back and a grinding sound caused a surge of adrenaline to flow down his spine. He could not get up or move his limbs when the boat docked itself on the beach. The locals discovered him shouting and pleading for help. They took him to the clinic in town and the doctor brought life to one of his greatest fears. He had broken his spine in the fourth quadrant and, like all those who have had such an accident, was facing a life of paralysis. The doctor was gentle with the selection of his words. He had met Carlos before but now in the consulting room was forced to wear his professional game face.

"There are procedures," he said with authority. Carlos did not respond. His green eyes were transfixed on the medical chart, which the doctor had used to explain the destitute situation to him.

"His life," he thought, "was about to change." Uncertainty plagued his identity.

The months that followed were like a bad dream. The town threw pity at the demise of their beautiful son. Shopkeepers sent food to the family and visitors would be reduced to tears at the news of what had happened. Carlos appeared optimistic to those that knew him. He would make jokes and offer philosophical responses to their serious concerns. There was no peace in his character. Spontaneous and angry outbursts echoed from his lips when the pressure of his new reality became too much. Carlos had always felt the presence of an invisible audience, which took note of his every action. It was a feeling he could not explain but one that comforted him when things were bad. This blanket of love did not seem to be present since the accident had occurred. People gave him attention because of his unfortunate state of being. His faith was pierced and not even the comforting words of a priest could undo the burdens he could no longer carry.

Santorini is rumored to be the last known existing landmark of the lost city of Atlantis. It is a black volcanic island born from the earth in a time when magical things were possible and people worshipped the sun for its warmth. Only vineyard grapes can be farmed in its soil. It is a place of sheer intoxication. Carlos had spent his life investigating the caves and adjacent islands. Three kilometers west of Santorini is the island of Lamos. It was not inhabited by any of the locals but mythology had given it the reputation of being an island where God was found. Visitors went to witness the magnificence of the salty caves and bathe in the natural hot springs. Carlos hoped that if there was a god, he could find him there, somewhere amongst the ancient ruins. He had spent one-and-a-half years of his adult life praying for a solution. It had not come to him in that time so he had decided to go in pursuit of his own resolution. His friend George promised to take him to the mystical island at the end of the week – weather permitting.

The boat ride took an hour as tourists ogled over the sights. It was an alien experience for Carlos to be seated at the rear of the ferry. He brushed off the queries of the passengers with a nod and a smile. George helped his friend onto the beach and escorted him slowly to the main cave. The deep and humid hole in the earth reverberated the sounds of excited laughter and camera flashes. The two young men rolled further into the stomach of the cave. Not a word was said until they had reached their isolated and private destination at the furthest point from the entrance. Some of the tourists had attempted to follow them, but they lost interest along the way.

"Is here ok?" asked George patiently.

"Ephgaristo," replied Carlos. George turned around as if dismissed from his duty and walked out holding the damp walls as he left. Carlos sat in his wheelchair in the dark, listening to the droplets of water falling to the ground. He had imagined that moment being more interactive in his planning.

"Please God," he said, "Don't abandon me now when I need you the most." His words lingered and then slowly faded. "I have been a good man all my life. I have obeyed your laws and helped those who are lost to find their way. I need you to help me get my life back. Please forgive me for my misdeeds and make me whole again." There was no response as he waited. "If you can't answer me, then please send me a sign?" Carlos looked at his wristwatch while the minutes passed by. He turned off his flashlight and driven by frustration, began to yell out. "If you won't acknowledge me, then I renounce you! You are not just and good!" Tears fell from his face and landed with the droplets of the cave. "From this day forth, I will see you only as a human-made symbol, a manufactured invention of wishful thinking." These words had used up all of his strength and breath. Being ignored is the most draining of insults.

"Don't do that," came a plea from a female voice behind his chair. A bright light had illuminated the corner of the cave. Carlos was frozen with terror as he turned to face his caller.

Hesitantly, he motioned the chair 180 degrees. The voice belonged to what appeared to be a creature of angelic proportions. It had the figure of a girl, about five feet tall with strawberry blonde hair and sunflower designs in her eyes. She was not clothed but a tranquil green glow outlined her female figure. The transparent wings that protruded from beneath her arms and extended beyond the length of her body defined her. She was not pretty like a picture of a fairy tale creature. She was as beautiful and mesmerizing as an electrical storm that forms over the sea at night and tears holes in the sky. Her words were like liquid as they dripped over Carlos. It was the meeting he had always prepared to have and now he was speechless in her company.

"Who are you?" he asked without thinking.

"I have many names and you have known them all," she replied calmly. She moved closer towards him. His eyes bulged as she started again. "You can call me Nona," she said. His shoulders began to relax. No name would have fitted such a pure entity.

And besides, names can be changed but souls are designed to be faultless.

"We have been together many times before," she exclaimed. "I have been watching you grow into the man you are today, loving you from a distance." The angel paused to let him in.

"Why have you never shown yourself before?" he cautiously questioned.

"It is not allowed because it creates too much human confusion. The only places we can coexist in the knowledge of each other are in demarcated holy areas such as these." Carlos began to shake. Never before had he been confronted by such humility. A million questions soared through his mind and one came to rest on his lips.

"Are you here to take me home?" he inquired.

"No," she answered. "I'm here because a second was too long to wait." The light became dim in the cave. The angel's silhouette reached forward and kissed Carlos into oblivion.

In an instant, he was penetrated with all the wisdom of life and his role within it. He saw his past, present and future in her eyes. He witnessed the waiting room, the agreement, and he experienced the yearning for his soul mate by his side.

"I was supposed to marry Penny," he realized.

"Yes, that was the deal," she professed.

He shook his fists in the air. "But how could you let me choose a life of modeling, sadness, addiction and emptiness without love?" Carlos asked.

Nona blinked as if to pause before responding. "Real love does not know control and you didn't choose that life," she said. "You changed the contract without knowing why and now you are free of the illusion of happiness. True lessons are simple."

Carlos held her in his arms. "But you let me live while my heart was in heaven. A man cannot live without his heart," he cried.

The fragile being shared his pain. She stroked his long hair and rubbed his forehead with her cheek. It was at that moment that George returned to retrieve his friend. He stumbled across the two beings in a loving embrace and ran out of the cave screaming for assistance. When he returned with reinforcements, there was no-one in the depths of the cave. The only evidence that confirmed his babbling was a silver wheelchair and a broken flashlight, which had been used to engrave one word. The caption simply read 'love'.

The search parties did not find the missing persons but strange folk tale stories began to circulate through Europe. Carlos and Nona had been sighted on many occasions. She had been seen carrying her man to the natural springs and tourists had viewed her dancing amongst the flowers by the island peaks. The two had been found making love on the white beaches by the bay and the cave was renamed Lover's Cove. People had heard them speaking in the smaller tunnels on the outskirts of the land. They reported the last conversations being about eternity and a male voice confessed that he would commit forever to making his girl shine.

George had a sculpture made of the image he had witnessed. The white statue was placed at the highest point of the island. Touring couples hiked up to touch it in the belief that it would repair their dented relationships or increase their chances of conceiving a child.

The inscription remains unchanged.

THE END

Eternal love must exist but I have had trouble locating it despite my extensive searching. So be it, because when it comes, I will receive it with open arms.

Chapter 8 Advice

Very often, advice comes as a result of the kind leading the kind, but a person cannot be dragged into the reality of someone else. In a couple of years, I had lost almost all sense of independence. I could do nothing for myself except ask for the assistance of others as I tried desperately to keep my reality from them. It was not an easy task. Suggestions were the fastest to arrive.

"Have you tried this?" they would ask with adamant voices, as if adopting maternal roles.

The reply was always a despondent "yes" from my side of the fence, which was true. I had attempted every known remedy to man and all the past success stories did little more than rekindle a tremor of hope for my deteriorating condition. I was lost in my own trauma and persona. The days were long and the nights even longer. Disability tests the strength of character but pain forces the mind into shutting down and in a room full of people, I was the loneliest mind on the planet.

I repeated the words 'focus' and 'balance' in my cluttered head. That was all that I could remember from my wise moments and the techniques I knew to beat adversity. This was, funnily enough, the two skills that I could no longer possess in the company of others. People grieve and console in different ways but they all, at some stage, take on a critical and authoritative role of the healing process. I cannot speak for all people that have danced with their own mortality but I do know how disempowering these good intentions can be. First comes a feeling of childlike safety, and then an overwhelming sense of gratitude and finally the understanding that no one knows how it actually feels. Maybe this is because everyone leans on their limited body of knowledge to find solutions to certain things and in the centre of that knowledge is their own image. It has been virtually impossible for me to explain the emotion of lucid sadness that I have felt around others. The simple truths that dispel all of these misconstrued securities is that in most cases, the person concerned finds the solution, not the person with the most logical argument. Perhaps it is the risk of losing everything that drives them to the extremes of treating the situation as unique that makes it work. A classic example is that of smoking, which is by common standards not good for general health. Dispensing advice upon someone to quit when he/she is sick makes sense but not in all cases. I see now that the only way to stop the habit is by seeing that "quitting will not induce death or harm as a punishment". It is therefore neither useful nor needed for anyone's survival. But pressing issues that don't necessarily apply leaves everyone frustrated and stuck in their own opinions.

I tried to beat my disease with the agreed upon, accepted, tested and known treatments and in doing so, underestimated the authenticity of the lesson on offer. I put it in a box and let my own dealings with hardship take a back seat. The result was unsuccessful and of all the things or beliefs I was losing, I missed myself the most. I suppose I forgot to take my own uniqueness into account whilst calculating the battle strategy. There came a time when second guessing the outcome was not an option any longer. It was uncomfortably apparent that the greatest lessons in my life would contradict the ones that came before them. Inconsistency started to become an expected learning curve. I can now see that no two people are the same apart from their attempts to treat similar events as identical encounters.

Good intentions and kindness are entirely different in their personal motivations. I held my most personal of meetings with close friends in well-known watering holes. Stuart and I have spent countless afternoons deciphering the intentions of women who have had both sweet and compromised motivations. It was out of this prediction that the next story was shaped. It describes how easily our conclusions about gender differences and life deductions changed. The end is usually always equipped with a sensation of shock and doubt. These characters took a shot at making that mistake of assuming authority. Advice is extremely subjective. If it makes logical sense, it's probably wrong. Very wrong.

SHORT STORY

THE CURVE

Drawing by Michael Poulsen

"There are two types of curves that need to be understood; the small of a woman's back and the ways in which to beat the system. Are you listening?" asked Stuart with a beer cemented firmly between his fingers. The two men were speaking in the New York sanctuary known as Homeward Hour, and once again, Stuart was dispensing all the advice that day as the rain showered the doorway. He was talking with his friend and partner in crime – Karl Richards. Karl had just found out that his girlfriend was leaving him for a more mature partner. No amount of wisdom could pull him from the dark place that he found himself in that afternoon. A couple of vodka shooters later, the conversation had become desperate. Seether was singing Karl's blues from the elaborate sound system. "We've been here before, my friend," finished Stuart. Karl turned sideways so that he was facing his counselor.

"Maybe it would be easier if I was a sixty-year-old guy," he said jokingly. The bar was empty with the exception of an old man sitting in the corner with his eyes closed.

They were just a couple of friends drinking in the middle of the day.

"Why does it always come to this?" asked the injured man. Stuart remained silent. "I mean, it's the same thing every time, just with different women."

Karl bit hard on his lower lip. He usually did this when he was angry at work in the advertising agency and it was a sign that a storm was brewing. Stuart knew the tell-tale mannerism from their time at university together.

"The only way to deal with Karl when he's like this is to let him vent," he thought.

"I'm twenty-six years old and I have committed my life to trying to satisfy the needs of every woman that has been with me. I have been strong for them, sensitive and successful, and for what? To be accused of being immature?" Karl was finished raging. It was more a plea for sympathy than an actual question. Americans don't sympathize, they rationalize, and it was Stuart's turn to come up with some answers.

"It's not their fault," he began "women don't know what they want and that's why they come and find us."

Karl listened tentatively to the logic and Stuart continued. "Maybe it's the extra chromosome or the years of suppression, but they look at us with both contempt and trust."

"That's a contradiction!" shouted Karl.

"That's exactly right and that's what they want, just like the book *Spin the Bottle* says – the excitement of ambiguity and it is up to us to give it to them," Stuart closed with a type of surety.

Karl had a pained look on his face and his friend could almost see the words processing in his head. Only accusations can save a man when he has lost a fight. "That's easy for you to say, Stuart. You've always had loads of women; I've never seen you have love problems." He was correct in his assumption. Karl had not seen his friend in emotional turmoil over a girl. They had been acquaintances for over twelve years and the shoe had not ever been on the other foot. Stuart called to the barman for two more beers. The bartender was in his late twenties and was an avid observer of the human condition. His name was Greg and he had spiked-up, jet-black hair and sharp features. This type of verbal honesty required more drinks and Karl counted the seconds until his comforter was ready.

"I have learnt to keep myself out of reach," Stuart said choking on some bubbles. He banged his fist on his chest and continued. "I got burnt once and swore to avoid the social trap of idealism. You see it all over movies, in songs, magazines and advertising. These things promote a system that only accepts a certain type of person or relationship as complete when all the point-by-point criteria are met. I mean, if Hugh Hefner or Madonna say that stuff, then that's fine, but they don't . It's some intellectually hyperactive, bored person that buys into the idea of sexual manipulation and then gets the rest of society to try and subscribe to it too." Karl wanted to add to his friends disapproving words but they were getting louder and fiercer. Stuart worked in New York City as an estate agent so he knew the gravity of his conclusions.

"Ten ways to make him yours, eleven ways to make her moan – it's insulting. Why don't they portray the truth?" he said, slapping his hand on the bar counter. Men want to be put first and so do their women," Karl quickly interjected. "So it's a power struggle – even I know that," he professed.

Stuart leaned forward as if to tell him a secret. "No it isn't. It's the communication that both men and women use in order to find confirmation. Men want to be seen as strong in the eyes of their women and they in return want to feel exclusively appreciated. If the magazines were honest for a change, they would locate the female G-spot between the ears rather than between the legs."

The barman dislodged himself from the back of the bar shelves and was nodding profusely.

"The male heart is not accessed through the stomach, but through the ego. Men require variation because they believe the grass is always greener on the other side, so women must be creative in their efforts," Stuart continued.

"And men?" asked Karl.

"Men," sighed Stuart for a second, "must acknowledge that girls have a small box of ideals in their heads. They all have one, and in it is an image of an adored and appreciated woman."

"So how do you beat the curve with your ladies, genius?" asked Karl sarcastically.

"Well, I beat the system by using contradictions as my ally. I simply let the woman attribute whatever meaning she has locked inside her box of ideals to my words." Karl needed a more specific example if he was to understand. He was confused and interested, but at least he was no longer worried about his own problems. Stuart was happy to clarify his outburst. He did it with the use of one sentence.

"I'm not ready for a commitment right now, but I can't wait to see where this thing goes with you." Karl stood up and lifted his arms to signal his liberation from depression and his new-found understanding of the female logic. He seized the opportunity to add one last comment. "What you say to women is a form of advertising; it's an invitation to do business. It's up to them whether they buy into it or not."

The two men were on their feet and bounced across the bar stools.

A voice of reason has existed since the first drink was ever publicly served and the first head of hair was ever cut. This barman was no different to his predecessors. He slid across the bar like a pint of beer in a classical western saloon. "Sounds like you guys have got everyone figured out?" suggested Greg.

"No, just half the population!" replied Karl proudly.

"You see that dude at the end of the bar?" asked Greg with a half-cocked head.

Karl and Stuart looked over at the motionless old man. The voice of reason carried on. "My boss says he's been coming here for twenty-five years, each time with a different lady friend on his arm." The two customers looked impressed while the barman took a breath to conclude his thought. "The thing is, I haven't seen anyone with him in my four years of working here, but maybe we can get him to tell you how he did it."

He walked over to the old patron. "Hey old timer, I have some people here that need your advice." The man's light blue suit was immaculately preserved as his forehead balanced gently on the wooden surface. The man didn't move. In fact he wasn't breathing either. The old man was as rigid as the bar stool that supported him. The two remaining customers were hit by the lightning of an unforeseen circumstance. They covered the deceased man with a tattered cream blanket and searched through his pockets for any signs of his next of kin. There was a wallet and a collection of foreign coins in his trouser pockets. The leather wallet did not contain any contact details. It was, however, filled with a stack of old Polaroid photographs – each one revealing a different and young, graceful-looking woman. His other pocket housed a single pair of navy blue, lace panties, which had an angel symbol printed on the front.

"Seems like this guy beat the system in his day," said Stuart.

"What?" replied Karl with a startled voice.

"The curve, it appears that he knew how it worked," Stuart replied.

The barman put the artifacts back into the man's pockets. Stuart spoke again to break the deafening silence. "I bet that one of those women in the pictures eventually caused this man to give up, bombarding him constantly with illogical behavior?"

The bartender could not listen to Stuart's reasoning anymore. "Let me tell you guys one thing!" he shouted. "I hear people talking about heartache every day. They all feel like they can't go on, but they do. They reinvent themselves and change their beliefs about the game. This old Casanova did not die of a broken heart, he died of loneliness and no understanding of the female form or psyche could save him. The people I meet fall into two categories; mainstream and slipstream. Even the custodian of alcohol had a viable summary of life. You guys are mainstream in the way you try to put people into classifications and impress others with your logic. But no two people or situations are the same. It is the manner in which you treat others that counts. All dynamics are a myth and only drunken fools follow them."

"What good are memories if you don't have anyone to share them with?" questioned Karl sheepishly as he took a step away from his friend who was lifting a stale beer to his lips. He began thinking of his girlfriend and how he had never studied the curvature of her back and how he hadn't asked her what dreams she had.

The weather outside had changed. It was finally a clear day.

Chapter 10 The Bigger Picture

Getting lost in the moment of a bad situation is incredibly common and human. For me, it would happen when I was alone and gazing inward for the answers to my demise. Why things happen in the sequence that they do is a mystery to everyone at the time and only patience reveals the much sought-after conclusions. The micro view is all-consuming.

"Why me?" and "Why this?" are the first probing thoughts to appear. It was upon this mentality that I left the confines of inner turmoil and took a look at my situation through a larger stance.

"What is the larger meaning to my current hardship?" I asked daily.

It was from that angle that I began to view things through a different light but the truth was far from attractive. I scanned the day-to-day activities of others for signs of humanity and salvation, only to stumble across more scales of destitute people. Opportunism, manipulation and a lack of courteous activities were all around. I saw the world implode on itself through greed, the waging of war, the lies and deceit, not to mention the willingness to isolate the weak from the strong. It is virtually impossible to acknowledge these misdeeds when you are focused on what's directly before you and while I always knew of their occurrence, I assumed they were happening somewhere else. It is not a pretty picture to suddenly awake to every morning and I don't even think the transgressors are aware of the gravity that their choices have. The macro view of life is shocking to a perceptive onlooker. Someone from another planet would surely see them as self-defeating and viral. Nature is the surest of mediating forces to the struggle of man as tidal waves hit continents with disastrous outcomes. Fires surged through cities and burnt and left a mark of conscience in its path. The bigger picture seemed tragic and gloomy in comparison to my personal struggles. It didn't offer any support to my quest for an outcome. Focus on the bigger scheme of things was another myth because there was even less detail in that portrait. It was then that balance licked its eyes and reared its head. The elements were confronted by goodwill and sudden collectiveness as people were joined in an effort to rebuild what was lost to the inconceivable. Swarms of people ran to the aid of those affected by the natural disasters. The news was elongated with footage of heroism and generosity. Disaster had brought the true nature out of the animals.

My reality seized the moment accordingly. The futile promises from strangers to give aid materialized and I was once again lifted into the limelight. Letters, phone calls, media coverage and prayers poured in as I tried my hardest not to let them be scrutinized by my wavering faith. I left for Holland on 8 June 2005 with my optimistic angel and a bag full of money raised by my friends. Our goal was to attain the healing properties of stem cells that promised to rectify neurological damage. The company, who administered the stem cells, assured us that the fortune spent on the therapy was a necessary and hopeful move in the right direction. Suddenly words and gestures carried some weight and we departed on the first available flight overseas.

The people in Holland are the exception to the usual malicious nature elsewhere. They were accommodating and helpful, helping me gain access to venues with the wheelchair and making me feel whole again. Nona and I sat in the middle compartment of the train to Eindhoven where the doctor and a complementary treatment awaited us. Transporting two bags, one disabled person and an array of medication is not easy on modes of public transport. The travelers rushed past us as they moved across the platforms. Nona was buried in luggage and shifted her attention onto her incapacitated partner before the final whistle was blown. The commuters saw her struggling to move the goods and most of them waited patiently for us to stumble out but one man took the initiative and offered the words "get on" whilst pointing to his shoulders. He wasn't taller than four-and-a-half feet, a sort of garden gnome with a confidence of a gentle giant. I locked my arms around his neck and he carried me out of the busy carriage. Without so much as an introduction, he was off after a single act of kindness. The spontaneous gesture had some of the other passengers follow suit and they moved our bags out for us. It was a nice renewal of faith in the human spirit after what felt like a lifetime of selfishness. We rolled onwards to our overpriced hotel three kilometers from the electromagnetic clinic in the woods.

Eindhoven is the fourth largest city in Holland and it is engulfed by the sounds of bicycles and church bells. We were just happy that it was so flat and all the facilities were equipped with wheelchair ramps. The treatment commenced the next morning under the guidance of the stem cell doctor, Dr Trommel and the expertise of the clinic owner and treatment inventor, Dr Essaidi. They discovered each other when Dr Trommel fell prey to an eye disease that was destroying his professional and personal livelihood. The treatments had restored his sight a few years earlier and the young Dutch doctor believed it to be the perfect accompanying therapy to stem cell implants. The rapport and common respect between the two medical practitioners was evident from the first glance as we entered through the glass doors. On the other side, was a series of metal rooms that pulsated and groaned as they operated. Dr Essaidi awaited our arrival and, with the help of his interpreter, motioned us into his consulting room to explain the procedure.

He was a bulky man, in his early fifties, with a healthy complexion and a warm character – a sort of young Father Christmas-looking man who exuded a self-assured belief in himself. The doctor was happy to meet us. Soon after our introductions, we were guided across the room and told to remove our clothes and proceed into cabin number four. We entered and closed the mirrored door that contained the smell of herbs and steam. The inside of the cabin was like the set of a science fiction movie. A padded metal bed lay in the centre of the reflective dome. The cylindrical room had the potential of a structure that was about to take off at any moment. We followed the prompts that came from the intercom on the wall. A few minutes later, we were surrounded by a claustrophobic influx of heat and pressure.

The first session lasted fifteen minutes and after a well-earned cold shower, we found ourselves preparing for the next round. It was not easy to endure the therapy for the next five days without a break. Heat is a catalyst for my condition and the process leaves its patients feeling as exhausted as the participants of a marathon race. But the third day had the added benefit of having the curing properties of stem cells put into my body. The miraculous injections were implanted intravenously, subcutaneously (into the stomach) and beneath the surface of the skin in my skull. The following morning, I walked assisted up a small flight of stairs.

"Was this the placebo affect we had been waiting for?" I thought hesitantly as we planned our new futures. Only patience and persistence would know the answer to that question. My mind, however, could not wait and I began conjuring up a story about an ambitious scientist who set out to rid the world of disease. This is his story and the obstacles I imagine he would encounter. It shows how prophets and revolutionaries are never welcomed and are ostracized by man.

I really hope that I could be such a great man.

SHORT STORY

THE NOBLE SCIENTIST

All Dr Makein wanted from life was everything. Years of scientific research had led him to believe in his educated decisions about health. After all, they had been tried, tested, analyzed and readdressed in every major laboratory in St. Petersburg, Russia. His field of expertise lay in the new discovery of cellular reactions to magnetic frequencies. The young scientist labored diligently at his desk and witnessed the affects of different frequency waves on cellular structures in order to investigate the viability of using them to create new medical treatments for untreatable human ailments.

Quantum physics supports what Russian intellectuals have been qualifying and claiming since the early 1900s. It now proposes that things are not as they seem. Not only that, but matter as we know it, is not solid at all. It is actually a combination of vibrating particles that form a cluster frequency, which interacts with other existing waves. Dr Makein suspected such a hypothesis with the greatest of ease because of his work in the lab, viewing the interaction that exists between particle matter and catalyst frequencies. He focused all of his attention on differentiating and identifying these patterns that cause the human body to change its behavior from a normal state of homeostasis to one of irregularity or disease. The results were easy to observe for the determined young scientist and he could think of nothing else at his home with his six children. Behind his impulse to convert confusion to meaning, was a genuine desire to contribute to alter the paradigm of medicine as we know it. The doctor's superiors were happy with his findings and they assisted him in finding a reputable sponsor that would further his quest to cure all sickness.

The middle-aged man found his direction through systematic trial and error after pondering the hurdle for many diseases. The solution came to him with a surge of genius. The headstrong inventor had been involved in much technological advancement over the years. One of these pursuits had led to the arrival and common utilization of the MRI CAT scan machine, for which he did not receive any credit or acknowledgement. The principles that the discovery was based on did, however, provide the insight for his big idea. He spent the bulk of his days speaking to himself and scribbling formulas on white boards until finally, his thoughts made sense from a scientific perspective. The proposed technology was, however, unreasonably expensive but the doctor would not let it go. In fact he could not leave it alone and he found a cosmetic company that supported his thirst for greatness.

In 1994, the two adamant forces began the unimaginable. They started building clinics that were destined to become the future of medicine for the human race. News spread fast and it wasn't long before patients were lining up by the hundreds to defy their practitioner's hopeless conclusions about their conditions. Even stepping into the clinics was like staring eagerly into the future. The cone-shaped rooms reeked of fresh herbs and electricity. Since autoimmune diseases had captured the paranoia and suspicion of the globe at that time, the experimental treatment attracted those who sought its salvation. This disorder, it turns out, was a relatively easy obstacle for the therapy to rectify. People entered his clinics overrun with regret and fear but they left a few days later, bewildered and relieved. Embarrassed and grateful, they signed the necessary testimonials and allowed the scientist to submit his ever–growing claims to the medical boards. At fist these reports were ignored by its recipients and dismissed as fantasy or exaggerated fiction. Dr Makein had pushed his fanatical beliefs through the gates of doubt before. All he needed was the scale of his findings and the authorities would be forced to take note of his genius. After all, extraordinary men were always insane in the eyes of their colleagues.

Makein Cabin Centres began appearing throughout Europe, each one building on the confidence of the doctor and adding to his legacy as the man who could cure the incurable. Data was captured and collected in the quest for the scientific revolution. The sponsors of these activities took ownership of the positive results and publicly congratulated themselves at every available opportunity. Verbal restraint is a fading commodity amongst the tepid. They had parrot-fashion learnt the dynamics of the machines and substantiated all their responses with an unfathomable comment by the inventor. The concept was easy to understand; a series of machines that heated their patients' body temperatures above sixty degrees Celsius (a temperature that destroys exposed viruses) coupled with the input of an invasive and opposing magnetic frequency to the illness itself.

News spread fast at the hands of the investigators. Skepticism was exclusively reserved for medical conventions in Moscow, until finally, one company took heed of the claims that the doctor had made. The afternoons were the favorite time of the day for him as he would drive his jeep through the cold, dark streets and reflect on the patients in turmoil that he had met that week. The streets were decorated with shadows and hidden cries. He left his concerns at the front door, by strict order of his wife Saskia.

"Worries," she used to say, "have no place in the home."

This was not always possible with six young adults in the house so Dr Makein used to prepare himself for the change-over from an acclaimed man of science to an understanding father. It took a few minutes for the household noise levels to take effect and the volume of Coldplay to be turned down, but one evening, a deafening silence had befallen the house. The dining room was host to his family and four unexpected new guests.

The unannounced men wore black clothes and stern expressions. They were representatives of the World Drug Administration and their visit that night was the result of a watchful eye over the doctor's activities. The intimidating men were members of the Medical Control Organization and they were at the house to reinforce their control over the development of all European medical research that is being conducted. The tallest man stepped forward and spoke sternly. "We need to talk, comrade."

Dr Makein turned to his family and uttered the request, "Give us a second alone."

His sons and daughters left the room with the three large gentlemen following closely behind and the comprehension that, even in Russia, capitalism reigns supreme.

"We need to speak, comrade. You are burning the hours too hard. If you continue, your body will eventually give up," said one of the dark men.

A tear rolled down the scientist's face. He knew their words were correct, but passion has its own requirements. He reached out and shook the hand of the shorter man. What transpired behind those closed doors will never be known. When the two men came out of the dining room, Dr Makein had lost his flustered red cheeks. The grey scientist watched through the window as they climbed into their black cars and departed. The young doctor had been coerced into agreeing to sign a restraint of trade with his new counterpart. This document forbade him from publicly releasing his findings for a period of twenty years, thereby paralyzing his hard-earned attempts to rid the world of diseases. The whole ordeal caused the doctor and his family to flee Russia and set up a new home in Germany where honorable intentions are valued and tolerated.

Money and fear drive people to seek asylum in places that they would otherwise have never chosen to be. Freiburg, in Germany, was a peaceful town to start over for all of them, but the scientist could not bury his thirst for closure. A few months after their arrival on a small patch of land by the church and school, a shiny clinic was erected. It was considered by many to be a clinic for the prevention of age-related illnesses, a modern fountain of youth. Not all the patients, however, were of veteran status. People arrived in wheelchairs and left standing tall.

The scientist was pleased with their recoveries and his own progress, even if no one was there to witness it.

Thank you – Без перевода

THE END

Chapter 11 Truth And Lies

The truth fits best between two points, and discerning which side of the fence it leans more towards, is usually difficult. Lies, on the other hand are engineered to deceive and it is very often the things that promise to bring the greatest happiness that yield the most damaging consequences.

I returned to South Africa with the hope of new ambitions and a fresh start, with legs that worked and a desire to live. The cells were in my body and it was time to construct my valuable dreams in the direction of beauty and finality. This was not the case. Lies had built the platform for another tragic letdown. It took another year to figure out how the deity thoughts interpreted those events. I wrote this story, which is about a person who got taken for a ride by an unscrupulous enterprise. It gave me little relief to write it although it made me feel less alone. Only those who have had their plans of normalcy shattered will know how it feels to be conned by predators that come to you as allies in the night. I pity their loss, and to the misguided attackers, I get no satisfaction at their inevitable demise. They should have known better than to wage war with a group of people that have nothing to lose. I imagined one of these people waiting to make things right.

SHORT STORY

THE INTERVIEW

An exhausted man held tight to his coffee while two policemen stood above him humming a tune from Red Hot Chili Peppers, who were serenading the inside of the outside room.

"Can you assure me anonymity if I give you what you ask?" said the captured man in a soft voice.

"We have been after these people for five years and we just want to know the truth," initiated one of the officers.

"My girlfriend is outside so you can't keep me too long, but here is a summary of the past two-and-a-half years."

"Just go slowly," urged the policeman.

"OK, the following is an accurate account of the past two-and-a-half years:

In March 2003, I noticed the first symptoms of my current struggle with Multiple Sclerosis (MS). I became aware of a change of sensation in my hands during a Sunday game of golf with my father. A few weeks' later, this numbed sensation started to have an effect in my toes and feet as well. It was coupled with a diminishing sense of balance in my daily activities. Walking up and down stairs became challenging and tiresome. I immediately pursued medical advice and had a series of blood tests done. The results all came back normal and my concerns were dismissed as anxiety.

In April 2003, I relocated from Durban to Johannesburg to start a new career in advertising. My mobility was deteriorating and I was worried I was becoming paranoid. It felt as though weights had been placed on my limbs, but without medical evidence, I persevered with my working demands. I began working with Princeton Promotions Pty. Ltd, a new company that specialized in talent placements with mainstream advertising. I did this under the premise and agreement that I was a co-partner of the company. My symptoms deteriorated rapidly and I was forced to sleep in the car outside between meetings. I booked an appointment with a neurosurgeon, Dr De Beer, in Carlton Park Hospital. He immediately recognized the symptoms and recommended a MRI CAT scan. My mother flew up to Johannesburg to give support. When I fetched her at the airport, I could not even negotiate the curb without falling over. My father flew up the following day. The scans came back positive for MS lesions in my brain and spinal cord. I was admitted into hospital for my first of many courses of cortisone treatments, which seemed to provide temporary relief, but the attacks re-occurred.

I continued to work six days a week, despite the recommendation from my neurologist, Dr Liebenberg, to slow down. He further suggested that I take Interferon medication at a cost of R8000 per month which was not covered by my medical aid. I therefore opted to go the homeopathic route, which did not yield any noticeable results. The Princeton business grew fast (1200% in just over two months). This was largely due to my involvement as both the spokesperson and the coordinator of new business development – the stress of which did, however, take its toll on my health. I borrowed money from my parents to purchase Interferon medication, the side effects of which were disastrous – raging temperatures and exhaustion in particular. Interferon is the accepted treatment for MS but I still sought further for a solution for a seemingly impossible situation.

There is no known cure for MS. I was not deterred by this prognosis, and refused to take it lying down. Therefore, over the next six months I pursued many avenues of western and eastern medicine. These included, *inter alia,* intravenous cortisone, homeopathy, acupuncture, magnetic therapy, iridology, yoga, spiritual healing, traditional African medicine, SCIO Quantum treatment, regressive memory therapy, frequency therapy and all western FDA approved (Rebiff 44) and non-approved (Lowdose Naltrexone, Histamine and bee sting therapy) treatments.

Things at the Princeton office/house became harder, much harder. My right leg became completely lame and the vision in my right eye became 90% blurred. Tension was building within the household after my girlfriend moved in and fought constantly with my alleged business partner. I was restricted to the house and could only pass from room to room by holding securely onto the walls. I knew that I could not continue with that lifestyle as it did not yield a monthly salary or promote healing. I moved out in the beginning of 2004 and was showered with promises of back-pay for my 12 months' service to the company. My girlfriend and I moved into a small apartment in Fourways, Johannesburg. I knew that something miraculous had to happen.

On a Sunday morning while trapped in bed, my girlfriend came home with the news of a miracle cure called stem cell therapy. She had come across it on the Internet and the evidence appeared so convincing that I was filled with hope and excitement. The R126 000 promised to me by Princeton, never materialized, so although hopeful, the problem had become a financial issue. I outsourced the services of one of my girlfriend's legal friends in an attempt to recoup money owed to me by Princeton. I followed the lawyer's advice and signed all the paper work. However, nothing was ever followed through by the lawyer.

I borrowed a wheelchair from the Johannesburg MS Society and pushed myself around the apartment trying not to end up on the floor. The muscle spasms and tremors in my legs had cut the circulation so that they were constantly purple in color. The pain was excruciating and I found myself in a hell like state. The high schedule pain medication had further turned my stomach into concrete.

I always considered myself very fortunate, especially with regards to the friends I have accumulated over the years. My girlfriend and I wrote a letter to these friends explaining the situation and the available cure of stem cell therapy. My friends responded immediately and they began to raise money in earnest for the guy who had never asked for any help in the past. I also contacted my parents and told them I needed help. Our combined efforts produced the required amount for the stem cell procedure, €16 000.

My girlfriend and I left for Germany on 16 June 2004. The night before we traveled, we both experienced paranoia about the validity of the treatment that we were about to undergo. The German-based company had advised me to stop all forms of medication, as it would compromise the effectiveness of the stem-cell treatment. I was in a ridiculous amount of pain, too much to even sleep a month prior to the commencement of the treatment. We arrived in Berlin and were instructed to appear at the Medical Clinic where I underwent high-dose vitamin therapy and preparation procedures for the stem cells. Dr Weiss was very kind and he reinforced that stem cells were the best option for MS treatment. (He has subsequently disassociated himself from FCT (Future Cell Therapeutics) and he is holding them accountable for FCT's fraudulent actions.) He recommended that I have Electro-Magnetic Therapy for a period of three days before he injected the cells. I followed his advice and traveled to Freiburg to start the Bisselli treatment the following day. Dr Weiss arrived at the clinic in Freiburg three days later where he injected the cells.

We recorded the procedure which took a total of twenty-two minutes to complete. I continued the Bisselli treatment for two more days before leaving Germany. I felt physically good and mentally positive for the first time in a year. I appeared to have more movement in my legs and improved motor control. I still did not have control over my bladder, but with the new cells in my body, I began a strict program of physical rehabilitation. The trip seemed a success and we attributed it to the miraculous stem cells I had received. A couple of weeks later I began to crash again. My girlfriend immediately contacted FCT and they said it was a temporary downfall due to the stress of traveling to Europe and back. According to them, the cells would only take affect one year later.

I set the goal post for June 2005 but once again I crashed. I therefore thought that it must be the environment I was in that was the cause of my demise, so a few months later my girlfriend and I moved to Cape Town, which always in the past had had a positive association and a sense of well-being. Broke and running on faith, we started to build a new life for ourselves, in spite of the fact that my deterioration was becoming noticeable again. I spent whole days confined to one room, alone, while my girlfriend pursued a new career. I ate in the kitchen, dragged myself onto the couch. I went to sleep in blood and woke up in urine. The depression that I experienced took its toll on my mental state and I found myself reaching for razor blades in the bathtub on a few occasions but could not follow-through with the action. My medical aid policy had come into effect, but our follow-up communication with FCT warned against all forms of medication.

FCT had attributed my deterioration to the fact that I must have been in the 20% of their clients that did not benefit from the cells. The only solution, according to them, was to undergo more stem cell therapy. My girlfriend signed a marketing agreement to earn credit for these desperately needed cells. We were both under the impression that the short-term benefits that I had previously felt, were due to the stem cell treatment. This was largely due to the bold claims that accompanied their guarantees and data. I did not have the funds for such an expedition. We began to communicate with Dr Bisselli and we learnt that the benefits that I had felt were not uncommon to this treatment! It took approximately seven more months to put in my pride even deeper in my pocket and allow my friends in Cape Town to raise the money for more Electro-Magnetic Therapy with Bisselli in Freiburg. It was during that time that a growth had formed at the base of my spine. I was checked into the Civic Hospital to have it surgically removed. The operation was complicated and the side effects disastrous. The money had been raised for a friend and I to go to the Bisselli Clinic and undergo treatment for a period of one month. My greatest concern was that I would not survive the two weeks prior to the departure date (18 June 2006). It was also a concern of my surgeon, Dr Smithers.

After I was released from hospital, some new information had come to light about the German company that we knew as FCT. My girlfriend and I discovered that they were not in Germany but in fact were based in Cape Town. We felt betrayed and I was particularly furious as these unscrupulous people were preying on vulnerable and desperate victims and they deserve their due punishment. We learnt of their previous indiscretions and fraudulent behavior, as well as their dubious associations with unsavory characters. I wrestled fearfully with the options of what to do and I felt that we alone carried this knowledge. Further investigation was obviously needed but I could not do it, given my state of health at the time. I contacted a local TV network because of their reputation for unveiling the truth and ethical misdeeds. I do fundamentally believe that stem cells are the future of medicine if administered by the right people. They would need, however, to treat disorders with:

a) an adequate volume not simply 1 ml at a flat rate;

b) honesty about their location and their company background; and

c) proof and validation of their past medical results.

The TV network started their investigations while I was in Germany for a month.

Stress is a very dangerous catalyst for MS attacks. The muscles in my throat had become constricted so I was struggling to swallow and breathe. I was completely paralyzed and my friend was worried I would not survive the flight to Germany. I did survive and improved after two weeks of therapy. I returned to Cape Town with a new lease of life, still unable to walk, but stronger than I had been for two years. I then went again to Germany with my father in September 2006. The treatment yielded the same results as in June. I completed the course of treatments in December 2006 and I now realize that the FCT stem-cells were at best, a placebo hoax."

"Well, that is exactly what we thought," said the other policeman whilst opening the door to the waiting room. "Sounds like hell!" he sympathized.

"Hell is a dark room without windows. These people sell fake windows," said the man as he left.

THE END

Chapter 12 Cures
(For Anyone With An MS Hurdle)

It is a common misconception among those fighting fire with sand that academics and experts are always the most knowledgeable of people in their fields. While this may be true for most industries, it is not applicable to all cases in the medical realm. It is more accurate to say that the sufferers or those most in need of a solution know more. A network of seekers exists behind all of life's major obstacles and within that grid answers are found. I was plugged into it very fast and instantly wanted to contribute to the cause. I wrote informative and up to date correspondence to the Multiple Sclerosis Society in the hope that we could all benefit from its circulation. Knowing what doesn't work is a positive step in the right direction to finding what does help. This is one of them.

In a nutshell

My name is Janji Slab. I am a twenty-eight-year-old ex-provincial tennis player, professional model and advertising graduate now living in Johannesburg.

A year-and-a-half ago, I didn't know what MS was or that approximately four million people world-wide were affected so much by its existence. What started as numb hands on a golf course and sporadic headaches, led to the loss of lower limb control and started a period of terror that threatened my lifestyle and sanity.

The type of MS that I am fighting is qualified by medical practitioners as primary progressive. My fight has been hard and sometimes desperate. It became apparent to me that the most debilitating part of this disease is its ability to remove all feelings of hope. I think that it is therefore due to the loss of options that a loss of hope appears. The MS Society has been a source of information and support for me. I guess the people who are fighting at ground level have always had the best understanding.

I asked my specialist if I was ever going to be normal again, and his response was "probably not". What he didn't realize, was that my constitution will not allow me to be normal or to take this lying down. So if you have just been diagnosed with MS and you are feeling hopeless, then these are some of the options available to you. I have pursued most of these and am currently doing whatever it takes to defeat this disorder. Maybe this information can help accelerate your recovery process and empower you to heal.

Cortisone

Cortisone is used to suppress the immune system and hold off attacks in order to let the body repair damage to the myelin sheaths. Intravenous and oral cortisone can be affective but they generally only slow down the attacks. It seems to be a short-term solution to a constant onslaught. Oral cortisone can be affective in maintaining some control over the attacks. Covacort seems to enhance the body's natural cortisone levels. The risk of these treatments includes damage to the spleen and liver as well as a lowered resistance to bacteria, allergies and viruses. A notable side affect is water retention and moon face. Water retention pills are advised to combat this problem, but be warned, you will urinate constantly!

Interferon/Betaferon

It can be helpful. It reduces attacks by approximately 30% in some cases and can help sufferers with relapsing remitting type MS. It is expensive but comes highly recommended by neurologists. The negative side, apart from the fact that this medication offers absolutely no hope for a cure, and the extreme cost involved, is that there are side effects. When I took it, the nurse who came to teach my girlfriend how to inject it into me told us that mild flu symptoms would be felt for the first few applications (injections are administered every second day). I felt violent side effects; extreme temperatures, paralysis, blindness, severe pain and really bad tremors. These side effects, in my case, lasted for three months; eventually I stopped taking the medication because it actually made me worse. Chemo treatments are available; they are less costly, less frequent and have similar results.

Cell food and N-code

Cell food oxygenates the cells and encourages them to function correctly. N-code aids neuron transmission. It is a good complementary supplement but will set you back R700 per month. Hydrogen peroxide is a cheaper alternative at R28 per bottle but it is important to remember that over-oxygenating your body can cause damage to the organs and cells. Another option is black onion seeds, commonly known by Indian people as kulanji seeds. It is well known for its oxygen properties and positive uses with arthritic problems.

Low dose Naltrexone (LDN)

50 mg doses of LDN are used to treat heroine addiction, research has shown that in lower doses, 4.5 mg, helps treat MS and has positive results in over 96% of cases. It is recommended that LDN be taken in conjunction with vitamin B12, Ginkgo Biloba and a multi-vitamin.

LDN comes highly recommended, and has had huge success with people with relapsing remitting MS. It is available in South Africa for R100 per month, and the doctor who imports the LDN also provides his patients with the supplements at a much-discounted price. No consultation is necessary, and the medication is sent to you via overnight courier. It couldn't be easier. And there are no side effects.

Procarin

Procarin is a treatment being researched in the US and the UK; it consists of histamine and caffeine. Histamine has been used for years as a treatment for neurological disorders with a lot of success. It acts as a neurotransmitter and enhancer; combined with caffeine it has been very successful in the treatment of relapsing remitting MS. There are no long-term studies to show what the effects a few years down the line are, but it looks positive. Unfortunately, the only component of procarin that is completely unavailable in South Africa is the histamine - we have searched and cannot find it anywhere. Procarin is administered as a trans-dermal patch that is applied to the skin. There are no side effects and the combination is easy to make at home. We have managed to find a company overseas who is willing to send it to us, and a doctor who is willing to make it for us and at a very low cost.

Homeopathy and acupuncture

Acupuncture is an Eastern medicine and can be effective in treating pain and cramping associated with MS. Homeopathic medicine is natural and aims to balance the energy systems/meridians of the human body. It is a subtle form of medicine and can prove to be costly due to the volume of tablets and drops required to treat conditions such as MS. I had a limited degree of success from this treatment. The problem with using this type of therapy, is that it often aims at boosting the immune system. Although MS patients have compromised immunities, raising the immune system can make it over-active and therefore more harmful to the individual concerned.

San Pedro (the four winds) and Ayuwasca (vine of death)

These two hallucinogenic roots and herbs are used in South America to treat ailments, specifically ones caused by autoimmune dysfunction. They are very powerful and controversial methods in this regard. They are, furthermore, only legally available in South America. The reason for this is to avoid over-charging and health risks associated with the mescaline type of practices. I met a so-called shaman who assured me that these herbs could undo my problem. He turned out to be one of these con-artist type characters and I only got to try San Pedro for an evening. The physical result was a trance-like state and aggressive muscle spasms throughout the experience. Please attempt these practices with a degree of caution because they may have an adverse effect on your mental faculty.

High dose vitamins

The vitamins were run intravenously into my body. Vitamins in large quantities have been known to yield interesting benefits to those who are unwell. I attempted this approach through a practitioner who believed in its properties. The supplement is run intravenously into the body. The MS cocktail consists mainly of vitamin B and the pungent after-taste is the only unpleasant side effect. Some people have reported drastic improvements from this therapy but there is an active placebo effect at play. MS sufferers are deficient in the presence of this vitamin so it helps but doesn't cure as far as I have seen. It is therefore ongoing and expensive

Apricot seeds contain vitamin B17, which is rumored to destroy damaged cells and is a natural form of cortisone. It is reported to be very effective in the treatment of cancer-type disorders.

The Journey

Brandon Bays devised a treatment, called *The Journey*, for all human ailments. It works on the system of consciously traveling into the body and isolating the emotions that caused the onset of the disease in question. This method has worked wonders in dissolving tumors and doctors are confused by their patient's impossible recoveries. Take care in the selection of the practioner as he/she can adversely affect the treatment's effectiveness with his or her own judgments. It is worth trying if you are emotionally equipped to handle it.

Bee sting therapy

I have not undergone bee sting therapy. Some people have had success with it. The positive effects of this treatment are felt for up to three months after administration. Four or five visits are required per year. It is possibly the histamine that assists in the recovery process.

Iridology

Iridology diagnoses and treats people through the close analysis of the eyes and retina, to identify traumas and diseases. The treatments vary but one is commonly used. This remedy is based on the eradication of the body's acidity and often includes the introduction of heavy metals to the body.

Alkalinity

This remedy is founded on the belief that when the body is alkaline it will function perfectly. A Candida diet (no sugar, dairy or wheat) is highly recommended. You can take base powder with water to ensure your body's optimal alkalinity. Acidic fruits and vegetables are to be avoided..

Colloidal silver/gold

Pure silver is considered to be nature's antibiotic. It boosts the immune system and can be applied topically to treat skin conditions. Some doctors believe that MS is caused by a dysfunctional gall bladder and liver, which causes the body to stop producing gold. Ingesting gold supplements and a strict diet are often prescribed.

The SCIO treatment

The SCIO machine was designed by Bill Nelson and is used to treat many different chronic diseases. It works on the understanding that we all coexist as interacting frequencies. It is based primarily on quantum physics, which makes us holograms operating within holograms. As such, we all have a perfect frequency until it is affected by an outside (disease) frequency. Every disease resonates its own identifiable frequency. The SCIO machine isolates and finds these abnormal frequencies and then inputs the equal and opposite frequency into your body. This balances your body's frequency and therefore makes it function properly. The results vary as the machine operates on a subtle/atomic level. Treatments cost about R350 per hour session. Practitioners of this machine are relatively easy to find.

Stem cell therapy

This is a cutting-edge treatment and is used to treat people with MS, ALS, motor neuron disease, Parkinson's disease, spinal cord injury and leukemia to name but a few. The treatment has only been around for about three years. The results have been astounding. Stem cells are human cells before differentiation. They are extracted from umbilical cords and then reinserted into the human adult. The cells travel to the source of damage in the human body and become healthy tissue. This type of therapy is not endorsed by the American Food and Drug Administration. It is only available in Europe so you would have to travel there. It is costly (about R150

000 per treatment), but what price can you put on your quality of life? The hype and ethical debate surrounding stem cell research is largely due to the fact that it was first implemented by means of extracting stem cells from human embryos. Umbilical extractions are considered to be more ethical and moral. In South Africa, you have the option of enduring a stem cell transplant. This is a highly dangerous procedure as the stem cells are transplanted directly into the brain after the immune system has been collapsed through chemotherapy.

Neurosurgeons claim that stem cell therapy is only effective if the cells are activated and directed as to where to do their job in the human body. Short-term research claims otherwise.

The Essaidi clinic

Doctor Essaidi is one of the inventers of the MRI CAT scan and has devised a successful treatment in Holland for diseases such as MS. This is a cabin treatment whereby sick people enter into a specially designed cabin that heats their bodies to eliminate free radicals and then puts an anti-MS frequency back in. This form of treatment has been successful in combating MS. When combined with stem cells, it has fantastic results. It stimulates the new stem cells into rebuilding damaged areas in the brain and spinal cord. One week of treatments in the cabin will set you back approximately R5000. The cabin treatment stopped my legs from having tremors after the third day. I could easily stand upright and I felt great.

Geopathic stress

Another thing to think about is something called 'geopathic stress'. Geopathic stress is stress caused by frequencies and energies being emitted from deep down inside the earth. If your home is built on a fault line, or a body of water under the surface of the earth, the energies emitted are coming into your home. These energies are not necessarily negative, but people with MS are more susceptible to them and are normally negatively affected. There is extensive information on the subject on the Internet. There is a doctor in Johannesburg and one in Cape Town that I know of who will check your home. They can do it from their computers in their offices so you don't need to worry about finding a specialist on the subject in your area. I strongly recommend if your home is built on one of these fault lines or water bodies, that you move, this energy could be seriously compromising your healing process.

Ritalin

Ritalin works in the opposite way to children for adults. It energizes me.

Glyconutrients

This is allegedly a potential cure for MS. Dealt with in Chapter 17.

Grape-seed extract and chamomile tea

A powerful antioxidant and a relaxing herbal drink.

Emu oil

Emu oil is a strong anti-inflammatory supplement and the effects are felt almost immediately.

All of these treatments are written from my personal experience and is therefore only my first-hand opinion. Good luck in your attempts to regain a positive quality of life. Rest assured that you are not alone in your fight and that there are solutions available to you. If you need any information or help please don't hesitate to contact me or check out the website: www.neversurrender.co.za

Chapter 13 The Music Inside

Music has always been another form of escape for me. I unwittingly made a soundtrack to my own life by keeping my attention on what was music playing in the background of memorable events and instances. Hearing those sounds now, I remember heartbeats, smells, people and thoughts that were so powerful at those times. The sounds of REM's "Losing My Religion" gave me rapid eye movement because it is the first song I ever had on tape as a thirteen-year-old boy on the run. The happiest of these moments were solidified by the sounds of the Dave Mathews Band and when I hear them, I can distinctly recall what I was doing and feeling on that particular day when I was playing that song. Music is not a procrastination tool or a medium for amusement to me. It is a soothing balm for my psyche that brings a comforting perspective to my erratic chants. These markers are sensitive when they appear and they make even the painful periods that they unmask, seem valuable.

Sound can travel anywhere and it can carry a message that is only understood by the recipient. I suppose, in a manner of thinking, it is my mode of transport through time. People who have had a brush with death often recall having their entire lives flashed before them. Big deal! I have replicated this process by putting a play list of songs together that is the catalyst to viewing my own experiences again and again. Music is found in every culture throughout the planet. It is the relief and sustenance of entire clusters of dreamers. With that in mind, I opened my ears to the sounds of things past and present. It made me think of a special girl.

One song crept in and spiraled my consciousness to an opposite period where I was rejuvenated and happy in my surroundings. Writing anything besides a signature on your birthday is near impossible, but whiskey-induced writing is sometimes persistent. I wrote the poem 'Looking Back' late on the night of my birthday and read it with appreciation the following day. It was a nice thing to look at first thing in the morning and for the first time. It is an exercise in doing the opposite of what everyone wants sick people to examine. It is also what my Russian doctor refers to as "seeing the rose rather than the thorns". He is a wise man to recommend choosing bewilderment over scarcity in the face of turmoil.

POEM

LOOKING BACK
(For Katia)

I remember a time when nothing else mattered,
When the world was pure and there was a light in everything, in everyone.
The sun washed the windows and burnt the smell of lavender on skin.
The warmth of it all, the places too seemed to lose the days.

The rain came fast and the earth richer,
As it mustered a grin.
Unlearnt languages followed the nights and let lovers live, in those places.
Smiling lovers with the warmth in them.

The falling was great on the shield of friendships,
On those collections of souls and gestures.
The world was generous and nothing else mattered,
The absence it gave.

I cannot remember the time I watched the spinning wheel,
Saw the hands and smiled.
Or how many times I turned to the skies,
And begged for the warmth in me, in everyone.

But the melody was sweet, filling the holes,
It was so very, very sweet.
And these are the moments and sighs,
Of a drenched clear desert.

The horizon on the puddles,
This was the shimmer,
The reflecting glass,
When nothing else mattered.

Chapter 14 The Kitchen Sink

Best buddies

After the stem-cell conspiracy was exposed, the police and FBI took over the responsibility of bringing the offenders to justice. The last bit of involvement from my side was a television interview with a local broadcast channel.

"At least everyone knows the monster can be slain now," I thought.

But the battle was not yet won. Emotional outbursts were dominant and MS looked like it was going to be a hurdle that couldn't be cleared by me. I sent a text message to Stuart: "I need you bud."

"Cool my boy – anything!" read his reply.

An email was sent to my friends overseas telling them that I needed my boys to help out once again. My pride had been forced so deep into my pocket that I couldn't even remember what it was like to feel driven by a surge of self-preoccupation. I abandoned the pull to do it all by myself and opened my ears to the plans and preparations to go ahead without any punitive objections.

The first fund-raising attempt was coordinated by Nona in the form of letters and information from wealthy adults and strangers with priceless intentions. A man, whom I have never met before, Gerome, donated a large sum of money without hesitation or questions to the second attempt at fund-raising. I spoke to him shortly after and told him that my ego/pride was taking strain.

"One day, my boy, I'll tell you what I think of pride," was all he said. Generosity and pride didn't need to have justified a presence in the wise man's life and I aspire to share his mindset in my own life. My girlfriend, and one of my friends, Bryony, a girl sweeter than honey, and Nicky, a girl more savory than milk, organized a party at the nearby bar with the owner's blessing. So I went forward holding tight to my 'milk and honey', a delicious temptation for anyone on a strict diet! Bryony's parents showered me with adoring love. They donated money and even inspired their friend, Joe to follow suit. I then understood the meaning of the word 'kindness'.

The night was full of entertainment, live music, inspiring words and supportive laughter. The battle was half won by the end of the night. I just wished my friends from Europe could have been there to enjoy the festivities. With the celebration of their commitment, the efforts continued. I booked Stuart and I tickets to Holland for a month later. My body was adamant to throw some more curve balls at my progress and a pain in my lower back got infected and turned into a tissue growth that required immediate surgery. I had the operation and writhed in constant pain but refused to forfeit my trip to the Essaidi clinic four weeks later. The morphine helped blur the lines between torture and overwhelming gratefulness.

Stuart and I arrived in Amsterdam after an eleven-hour flight. We had arranged a taxi service to drive us to the clinic. My eyes had lost over 70% clarity so Stuart was leading the search. After an hour of wandering around, we spoke to a driver who was holding a poster that said MS Ganyie and Stuart. Stuart was under the impression that the 'MS' stood for Mrs! We apologized profusely and laughed at how easy assumptions can lead to potential abandonment. The driver was in his twenties, with the responsibility and language of a forty-year old. Somewhere in the diligent youngster was a curiosity that we saw surface each day when he transported us between the flat and the clinic. The month that followed was no walk in the park. Stuart watched over me closely and would repeatedly ask me, "Are you ok, my man?"

"Yes, I'm in that place," I would answer.

This translated to mean that I was neither here nor there, and that I didn't have the energy to care. A month later we left with a sense of personal accomplishment and a positive anticipation of things to come. The storm had subsided to let me breathe for a while but overseas, things were just beginning.

Alistair was leading the campaign to throw a fundraising party for 250 people in central London. Every effort was made, venue and entertainment booked, the invites were sent and the high bar was set. Alistair was well known for his inquisitive mind and gentle nature. He had poured that interest and gentility into his girlfriend for many years but they were like oil and water and could not mix. Marina is, however, a girl who's worth the fight. Josh and Brett helped with the preparations. They were both determined searchers and seekers of the unknown, waiting to make a valuable difference. Sean shared these sentiments, and he rose to meet all the requirements that were presented with a smirk and quick comment. Pippa was always there, as she had always been. A beautifully spirited girl who loved people for who they were, not what they did. She was a constant and always did a lot. An entire book could be written about these amazing people and the others that surround them but destiny will not wait for additional sentiments when it comes calling. I recall fond memories of our adventures together. Brett was a warrior, who would never back down from anyone. He had once lost his front tooth in such an encounter with a trouble-causer. A temporary tooth was installed and we were all at a party discussing his endeavors. He defended himself with boldness but his temporary filling exited his mouth and flew across the dinner table. "Guys, where's my tooth?" he asked with his top lip folded over.

Sean seized the opportunity. "Tooth, you can't handle the tooth!" he cried.

We were just a few good men. Those were good times to be alive. Close friends are like a great and rare bottle of red wine. They are worth the wait, worth more than their weight in gold and worthwhile enjoying in any given situation; the illusive fact is like a ghost in the fog: what you feel is who you are.

Chapter 15 Miracles

After deciding to throw everything, including the kitchen sink at my healing process, I returned to my girl and house in Cape Town. The physical improvements were massive but I still couldn't walk or see on my own. It took a few days for the environment at home to become intolerably difficult. Arguments ended most of the conversations and the quest for a miracle was still looming. There is a comfort and protective shield that only the home environment can provide. I reserved a flight back home to be secure in the arms of unconditional love. I had previously considered this move to be one of resignation of defeat because of my troubles. Now it gave me a warm and peaceful sensation. I think it had always had that association whereas everything else was, at best, temporary. These realizations come without warning and this part is written in real time.

Impermanence will set off worry and panic in the minds of most thinkers but in my case, it excreted an acceptance of things as they were and the speed at which they were unfolding. It is more accurate to say that I was harboring deep-seated desires for an easy way out. A promise is a promise, the yardstick of finding the spark that would give me a chance of locating my resolution and answers. I had sworn a long time ago not to take the easy option out of this life, no matter what happened. The best foreseeable solution was the long awaited arrival of an all-seeing being and Father, the occurrence of which could bring a spontaneous healing amidst a hopeless backdrop. A helpless situation is one that can pass, given the right stubbornness and character but a hopeless perspective is a downward spiral without a tangible exit. I tried every day to not visit that site for fear of not returning from it. I became pre-occupied with lighting the fire that would welcome the appearance of miracles.

"Miraculous phenomena need to be given the same respect as the problems themselves," said my father in the family lounge. I needed to take note of the important equalization period involved in turning situations around.

"I would appreciate it if they could come soon and without warning," I replied. "That would be a nice surprise."

"They will," he stated clearly while eating his dinner.

I conjured up another short story to accelerate the inevitable, but real miracles cannot be activated by cheap tricks, otherwise patience would not be required. I included Genevieve, a close family friend, and she was a good support to me in a time of need.

FICTION

THE MIRAGE

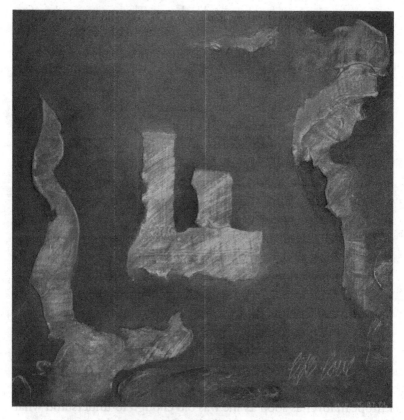

Painting by Nicole Smuts

France is infamous for women who make a living out of turning tricks but Genevieve was an exception because she did exactly that. The twenty-five year old Mauritian girl could pull a rabbit out of a hat and make it vanish before the crowd even had chance to cheer. Her sleight of hand tactics gave her a spot on the Paris calendar as the magician who must be seen during National holidays. Her performances took place in erected marquees that were decorated with silk drapes and sultry candles. This gave her acts an authentic appearance and set the scene for her to use smoke and mirrors to hide her secrets.

She was a wholesome-looking girl with brown hair and eyes, soft skin and a warm smile. Her thirst for adventure caused men to gravitate to her late night shows. The most sought after magic feature could be witnessed on the night of the Bastille Day celebrations when the French celebrated their independence from monarchy. The activities of that specific day were full of drinking and shouting at the top of the lungs. And while grown children were reborn, Genevieve set up the stage for another great show. Her mother had repeatedly told her that she was destined for an unorthodox life, filled with mystery and wonder. These were valuable bedtime stories on the island of Mauritius where she grew up but the big bad world did not support her mom's belief in the wondrous and sublime. Genevieve's dad had been raised in France and his nostalgic stories caused the young girl to leave the sanctity of the small island in search of a life less ordinary. Intrigued, fearless and armed with a large capacity to love, she arrived in Paris with no long-term plan in mind. She could at least speak the same language as the people there, even if identifying with the abrupt locals was difficult. The young and naïve girl packed a pocket full of postcards and scouted the city for memories. The Eiffel Tower was at the top of the list and it was there that she met adult temptation, Jean-Paul the Great.

Genevieve's mom had always said that she should have a European lover as soon as she was old enough to understand what those words meant. Jean-Paul the Great shared her sentiments and when he met the traveling teenager, he wooed and impressed her with his trade. He was a street magician who busked and performed tricks for the tourists at sought after sites. He wore the usual magician attire, a red lined jacket with yellow cubes sewn onto it and a full-length black cape. The man's tattered blonde hair hung out below his top hat. Genevieve placed €5 in the wooden box by his feet and stood back to watch him work. He seemed pedantic in his movements, shuffling cards and folding paper to please the crowds.

"And now," he said lifting a case to his shoulders, "we shall appease Jahzareth by turning this cardboard box into a flock of birds."

The viewers of the spectacle watched in disbelief as the square case was transformed before their eyes into seven white pigeons that flew off on release. Genevieve watched the final act from a cross-legged position. She approached the wary magician as he was preparing to leave.

"Bonjour," she started, but he was too busy packing up to notice her inviting stare. "That was wonderful," she continued.

"Merci," he replied over his left shoulder.

Their eyes met and they were catapulted into a love affair that only they shared. Over the next few months, it was not all they collaborated on.

Genevieve would watch her man mesmerize audiences and at night they would enjoy wine and fine cuisine with the secrets of how Jean-Paul achieved his feats. After a few too many glasses of French wine, Jean-Paul would relay to Genevieve stories of the unfamiliar. He told her about the all-seeing, all-knowing ruler of magic-Jahzareth. He had heard of the symbols' power through his apprentice as a boy.

"Jahzareth makes everything possible," he would say.

Genevieve did not truly understand his ramblings, as it is difficult to understand the words of a man who has consumed too many bottles of the good stuff. She did, however, take conscious notes of all the tricks that he had taught her and on a usual Sunday show, she made her debut appearance as Jean-Paul the Great's assistant. The increase in audience-size reinforced Jean-Paul's confidence in her abilities. All was content for the young girl and her magician boyfriend, until one afternoon after her waitressing shift at the restaurant, she returned home to find her boyfriend training another assistant in their bedroom. It was the end of, not only a partnership, but of a performing duo as well. The heartbroken girl stewed over the night's events for many weeks but she was adamant not to return home just yet and one day, while re-enacting a magic trick for a young boy, a crowd gathered. Genevieve decided to become the magician that she thought her ex-idol was.

Her shows were distinctly unlike her teacher's. She expanded her tricks through hard research on the Internet and her collection of books about illusion. The novice trickster did draw from and upgrade many of Jean-Paul's methods. She had, for instance, used the usual words of magical supremacy but instead of pigeons flying from the concealed compartment, doves were employed. Genevieve got a sense of retaliation on Jean-Paul with every display. He had tried to win her back once he had discovered her movements.

He even tried using the guilt of what he had taught her in his arsenal of excuses for temporary insanity. But not even a Ben Harper compilation could help him to convince her of his innocence. Selfish people always consider themselves to be over-generous and it feels to them like a well-earned vacation from reality. She ignored his attempts at deception and four months later was the long-awaited Bastille Festival. Genevieve got to her location early in order to set the scene without any of her potential members being exposed to her trade secrets. As dusk fell on the Arc de Triomphe, so did the eager participants of the night's activities. A good turnout was all the girl set her mind on.

Genevieve selected her words well that afternoon and she breathed in the scent of expensive fragrances as she squinted her eyes to emphasize her performance mystique. The eyes are the most expressive of organs. An hour-and-a-half later, it was time for the magician to finish up and, as usual, the last trick held the greatest impression.

"And now!" she cried with her arms extended to the flickering night stars. "To honor Jahzareth, in a second, we will rise up and take flight to reach him tonight".

This part of the show required careful planning and group participation. Three audience members were in on the delusion. They were secretive associates of the illusionist and when she asked the audience to close their eyes and imagine the sandy beaches of Mauritius, the partners were moved behind a mirrored screen. The remainder of the viewers watched eagerly as Genevieve announced.

"And now the power of Jahzareth will transport us to my home town for breakfast."

The three distanced friends held tight to the doves that would be released when the smoke bombs went off. Genevieve focused on a part of the beach that she would play as a child. She opened her eyes and with a sensation of peace in her heart, threw down the two small capsules that caused a gust of smoke.

The unforeseen and totally illogical thing happened. Over three hundred white doves flew out of Paris at 9:30 that evening. The surprising addition to that phenomenon was the spontaneous disappearance of over three hundred French residents that were watching a show by the city's famous landmark.

Language will sometimes find a way of having a presence in reality.

Genevieve added many new words to her shows on the shores of Madagascar. She included a new phrase in her last act before dusk:

"Be careful what you wish for, when real` magic is summoned."

THE END

Everyone has a manner of verbalizing their understanding of the truth. I carry a positive attitude in the company of others and I pray words will fall upon receptive ears.

"I must rest," I thought, "because no one can be ignored forever, and I am too insistent to be over-looked. My words were also too convincing not to be heard by the court, even if they are the result of an over-zealous imagination.

Another untruth is revealed in the belief that imagination is not essentially real. What a travesty to think that reality must be agreed upon for it to be considered true. I wonder how any of the great minds of our time would have reacted to such a limited view? Oh wait, they did face those obstacles. I don't believe in or trust 'the real'. It is boring and predictable. I believe in aberrations, things that defy the expected norms. They are exempt from being defined and they thrive on rebellion – the liquid sunsets of life.

Chapter 16 The Complete Sentence
(For Riana)

My sweet surrender did not come easily. I fought it at all costs. Autoimmune disorder means that the body needs conscious involvement in previously unconscious actions. Anything from chewing food, going to the bathroom to taking a step forward requires strategy and determination. Detachment from these tasks is often also needed and I put my mind on acquiring unimportant or additional information. I asked for the exact words of the perfect sentence that could put my concerns to rest and make the tortuous manageable. Helpful expressions can't be remembered, as every person needs different stimuli to feel comforted.

I met a woman named Alicia whose son had broken his neck in a motorcycle accident. Her approach to his healing process seemed to be working and she attempted to share her wealth of knowledge with others. Her boy's demise had become the system with which she valued herself. But, whatever her motivation was, she fell short on many occasions by trying to use the same tools and spiritual mindset to fix a host of problems that were ultimately different from her son's.

I searched for a sentence that was relevant to only my signature and current predicament. A type of verbal fingerprint that could remind me of how I felt inside but it was forced and the words that came out were said with a voice that did not match my own.

The environment at my family's house was comfortable and when I sat back in the acceptance of the fact that it was not going to happen, it came. It was like trying to retrieve a name that has been lost, which finally appears during an unrelated thought. It took me by surprise, tapped me on the ears and brought forth another revelation.

"This is just where I am right now," I whispered to myself.

There are always those people on any given flight that get nervous because they are not the ones flying the plane.

This short sentence made me feel the enjoyment of traversing aimlessly through an unchartered path.

The line was complete and true.

Life and love are outside of my control, but within my reach.

Chapter 17 The Glue

What an emotional rollercoaster ride this has been. It has proved to be founded on a seriousness that almost seemed inescapable. Jokes became contemplative discussions, life and casual chats between friends turned fast into motivational talks. But emotion is the glue that binds us, and our experiences. The glue, however, melted, and took me on a spree of incoherent thought processes. This is ten minutes of such an endeavor taking place within my consciousness. My evolutionary process has, like the planetary natural order of things, been demented and cruel. It happened as fast as the biggest leaps in history before the dreaded asteroid was supposed to hit.

The number one comet of overwhelming emotions to crash into me was that of disinterest. It was masked beneath an avoidance scheme that didn't want to acknowledge the manner in which those before me had fallen and not been able to get back up.

"I am not like them," I would say and mean it.

But I was like them, worse off than those unfortunate beings. I just fought harder, because of my age and because I still had the memory of a mobile, limitless life wedged firmly in my heart. The glue flowed and forged a bombardment of feelings that I went to bed and woke up with.

I have put the old fear of mediocrity aside for the terror of nothing short of everything. It was the second emotion to flow through me until it was like falling asleep in a nightmare and waking up in a hell that did not know any mercy or humanity. There are no phases to suffering. They are as non-specific as diagnostic definitions, big names that need to explain to patients and their families over and over. There are only three variations or patterns that sick people adhere to and follow. The first is denial in the hope that the storm will just pass. The second is the fear that it never will and the third pertains to caring. It is the dissection of emotions into two: those who care what happens and those who, through so many tries, now don't give a damn. The transition from fear to anger is a quick and uncontrollable one. Anger promotes sudden movement and often results in survival in certain situations but I'll leave nature to figure out the thin line between being indomitable and unapproachable in most conditions.

It all came out and I got extremely pissed off at my family's home in KwaZulu-Natal. Sean was there, though. He is an old friend who everyone calls Fox. He became a great friend. Even when he's down, he is still dominating. The tranquil surroundings of KwaZulu-Natal could not divert my focus from one that was inward to outward. I just wanted to have options again, the choice to concern myself with insignificant things like what people think or what I did or didn't do on a given day.

"At least it keeps you alive," some would say, comparing my reactions with a third person perspective.

"Only to have another day of suffering," was how I wanted to respond, but that would have only brought on sympathy or a loss for words and made me feel worse. I sensed that "things could always be worse" was about to be used at those times so I would graciously change the subject. Still. I couldn't help but think that dreams and worries appear closer than they really are and when they are gone, who will even be able to remember them?

Another plan and more faith were needed, this time with a direct relevance to the glue that was holding me together.

"God is love and love is God," my mom would repeat when I slipped emotionally. I felt the influence of those words and set my sights on the next game plan, but first I needed to construct one to believe in.

I met with Chantelle, a middle-aged woman who is also afflicted by the random persecution of MS. She read about Nona and I in a magazine and felt compelled to assist us in some way. The news she carried was interesting and new to all of us - a sugar-based supplement that defies medical science. I started taking the powder solution that coats the outside of human cells, allowing for effortless inter-cellular communication to take place. Stabilizing emotional states is however another issue. I booked an appointment with a body-talk practitioner, the upgraded version of the reputable kinesiology treatment. It is geared at instructing the body to heal itself. The body is, after all, the greatest and most complex machine known to man - and it is alive.

The question then is: "If the body is the expression of the life force, then am I just a passenger along for the ride?" There is little peace in this thought that we are all pawns in a supernatural game of chess when we are the ones that feel each move. But I cannot shut my eyes to the way things really are even if it makes me question my own sanity. I have acquired knowledge and gathered information with every experience and accompanying change of sensation. Each one was an attempt at storage in case a similar situation ever arose. They amounted to a quest at insuring the pursuit of happiness or the avoidance of pain. So how does that translate to me now when pain is unavoidable? My muscles and joints ache constantly, my girlfriend doesn't tell me she loves me anymore, I see happiness in others and live in fear of myself. I know there is something else that exists behind the drawn curtains because I notice it every day. I cannot ignore the signs anymore.

I met a guy when I was younger who had lost his grip and was considered by psychologists and people who knew him to be insane. He spoke of signs and could not understand how we did not acknowledge them but the opening paragraph of any self-help or spiritual book agrees with his angles. They suggest that everyone should step away from what they think they know and experiment with new interpretations, especially about themselves. Maybe I am en route to Crazyville but there is only so much energy that can be spent in a day worrying about oneself before perception, however limited physically, takes over. What I couldn't deny was the constancy and importance of events. That is to say that they were meaningful in the long run … all of them. Balanced and enlightening, they were only significant in their entirety. They did eventually spell out a single truth. Everything is perfect.

There is precision in each and every thing that happens. Of this I am not mentally sure. I could be mad after all but I feel it with such strength that I could be deluded not to. Let me use a relevant example. I was born with a genetic disorder that was to eventually become detrimental to my happiness. My whole life was full of anxiety and concern, which the doctors say triggered the onset of my troubles. I always seemed to have a knot in my stomach for some or other reason and for the past couple of years, cursed that short-sightedness on my part. I found out today that muscle tension in the stomach is imperative to body movement as every directional change is anticipated by the locking of muscles in that area. The truth of the matter is, if I didn't live with an innate anxiety, then I would have lost bodily control at a much earlier age. I would never presume to tell anyone what to do. Figuring that out is the point to it all and totally subjective

What I need to do now is ascertain what emotions are beneficial and what are detrimental to my health. If I dissipate these things then they translate to one question: "What am I choosing between." Easy, right? Sometimes my choices cause the most traumas. Nona believes that everything is a decision with devastating consequences, each one a direct judgment on her character. She tries to show her inner attributes, which she is proud of, by insisting others see them. Although harmless and easily forgotten, they push good people away and keep them at a distance. It is the choices that she holds so dear that prevent her from truly being known as I have known her when she is defenseless and wonderful. She is constantly growing and working on herself. I just hope she gets there before she realizes that the correct choices are half luck. I decided to let these choices and people reveal them to me. The only gauge I have is intuition, not suspicion, to help them. I allow a gut feel to make my decisions. If they are the wrong ones, then I dismiss them as lessons or a temporary error. Either way, I am less exhausted

Triggers can be defined as the external catalysts to internal turmoil. They are a lot like the dog that bit you when you were younger and gave all pooches a negative association thereafter. They are very often undetectable to the person at the other end of the firing line. I just knew that there was something inside of me, tearing me apart. Finding these was near-impossible because I was desperate to blame someone or something, anything including myself, for my change of lifestyle and belief in justice. The rewarding part of my search inwards was the instant reaction that my body had to the tested emotions. I would often say that I used to be active, now came the realization that I am reactive and the tears and anger came rolling in unannounced.

The blatantly obvious one was fear of the unknown or of things of which I had limited knowledge. Underneath that surety of eventual punishment was a lack of self-confidence. It has always had a seat in my subconscious and spoke up when I was nervous of the outcome of any particular situation. The idea that we are being judged and served constantly is the most damaging and incorrect of assumptions because it is far off the mark. What about the more accurate view that there is an abundant energy-spring whose sole desire is to assist each and every one of us? That mentality is hard to digest. For me, that tasteless thinking lingered. It was at the base of my rationale and when things did not work out, I did not feel surprised.

Omens are accepted through both good and bad events until one arrives that can't be taken aboard. In my case it is obvious. The disappointment has come with every girl I ever cared about and every trip to the doctor's office. The doctors' visits were pre-empted by my mom's concern and her fear of physicians. The relationship pitfalls were my own doing. I have an ideal in mind, which I automatically superimposed the face onto the girl at those moments. I never learnt from this trend that caused an aching sensation in my heart. Now I sense the fundamental lesson manifesting itself.

My girlfriend is making a conscious attempt at finding herself while at the same time distancing that new person from me. Can't say I blame her but then she can't blame me for expressing how I feel. When I first met her, I was looking for something different to what sat beside the cactus on my desk. When our relationship became more serious, I had a few epiphanies and revelations about us as a couple. The warning signs took a backseat as our priorities changed. I loved her for different reasons and when each one was disproved, I simply replaced it with the next. It started by being intrigued with her relaxed manner, then her strength in hostile situations and finally her large capacity to love, which was directed at the author. The trait that closed the emotional deal in my heart was her dreaming potential and stubbornness and I was bewildered by it because I had never seen behavior like that in anyone but myself. Perhaps it did not disappear, but just expired. I wish her blissful happiness - wherever she finds herself.

Most unexpected events have a sell-by date and a course that gets run down eventually. The physical state I find myself in is following those guidelines. I do not witness them on a regular basis but I know they are there, waiting to be recognized. The utensils that are needed to make them feasible are in my past, unlike the problem itself. When I was younger, I made a bold tennis challenge on a player with a much higher ranking and winning record. His parents were shocked and verbal about their disgust at the ridiculous suggestion. My mom defended my request while they swore and cursed her publicly. She stood her ground and the match was scheduled for the following Tuesday afternoon in spite of the rage that it had caused. That day saw all of the complainants sit on the left side of the grandstand with sniggering laughter and sarcasm when the match started. My two parents sat alone on the right-hand side and watched the game. I won the match that day. In fact, I annihilated my opponent in straight sets for everyone to see. It comes out when the chips are down and it is the only possible ending. I will go to sleep tonight with the same words that echoed in my head that day on the tennis court when I had sweaty palms, my heart in my throat and my skin filled with electricity: "Calm down and stay focused because there is nothing in this world that can prevent you from winning."

Logical capabilities do not feature when you just know. They end just like all seasons and ultimately dispel stupid fallacies.

Chapter 18 Habits

Habitual behavior fuses the line between needs and wants because it becomes a learnt way of getting through the days without experiencing too much pain. There are those that believe the pursuit of pleasure and avoidance of pain are the two strongest intentions that navigate our every decision and make us question those very conclusions. But this method of thinking only directs me through a lonely path of assumptions, which is after all, a dangerous road. I predicted the third trip to Holland would yield an end to my nightmare. My father and I left on the last flight out of South Africa on an eleven-hour flight to hope and uncertainty.

We arrived in Amsterdam and followed the usual program and found our driver, Navid, who took us to our apartment in Eindhoven. The following two weeks were almost identical to the month spent there in June. I immediately started to conjure up images of how I would feel by the end of our stay.

The medical trip was broken by a visit from my grandmother who had come to see us from Germany. She and her husband prodded us with questions about the therapy's veracity and the practitioner's credibility.

"The website says that he is not a doctor," announced Gran with a look of accomplishment.

"I know, Gran, he's the guy that invents machines that doctors have to study how to operate," I said, without requiring applause.

The conversation drifted and turned into a History lesson about the family heritage. Gran was leading the class that evening as she is always happiest in the spotlight.

"It's a pity that all the people who know the most about the family are dead," she said with a defeated look in her eyes at the end of her lecture.

"I know, Gran, but you are still here. I don't want anything from you, except to know you," I said across the dinner table with a flash of honesty.

Some other German family members came to pay their respects the next day, although I suspect they were coming to prove their own conjectures. It's really paradoxical how the more we become communicative, the less we are able to understand simple notions.

My dad and I had no sooner become accustomed to our alien surroundings, before we were seated on a plane destined for our own continent. Some thoughts, however, had surfaced during our visit to Holland and I unwittingly packed them in my head-luggage on the return trip. Strange thoughts entered my field of consciousness under the stress of the non-invasive therapy. Awakenings or curses? I may never know, but the thoughts rolled in hard and furious. Struggling and fighting had taught me a few ways of altering my reality and physical difficulties. These came tumbling back into my mind as if to be renewed once again. It is the first thing a person that is on the edge of losing his mind realizes, that insanity is less scary when compared to real suffering. Any justification is, therefore, employed to keep the anguish at bay. The first of these rationalizations arrived with a ludicrous indulgence. It started with the acknowledgement of 'the little man' who is both the conscience and restricting voice in all of our heads. The little man tells us that not everything we dream of is possible. He is the negative, restricting voice that warns you not to parachute out of the plane. His advice is always taken seriously because those who have rebelled against it have ultimately found themselves wanting.

After a while, I stopped trying to prove him wrong and feared him as the voice of reason. This often kept me out of harm's way but as I found myself embraced by real danger, I decided to let the little man serve me for a change. The way I did it was easy.

His bantering had caused me to stop being grateful for things in case I lost them. His words of warning were always present at those moments and as it turned out, they proved themselves to be true. I therefore became grateful and expressed my thanks for the bad things that I was experiencing. The little man, full of ego, could not stop his interruptions even in those instances. Those defamatory remarks appeared as constructive and they pushed me in the direction of positivism. This coping method reached its expiry date just before we embarked on our journey home, but I had one eagerly waiting to fill its place. It was almost like a mantra or verbal affirmation and it was negative by nature.

By using three powerful words, I was able to retain my autonomy over the threatening situation I found myself in. This was done by adding the phrase "never, ever again" to the memories that terrified me. If I had spent a day in agony, I would recall it by saying "I will never, ever feel that pain again!"

Even good habits are hard to let go when they cling to my memories with sharp claws. The trip back was filled with self-reflection on the conversations with my dad, the time with Essaidi and our introduction to Nicholas and Teresa, an American couple seeking the expertise of the Dutch cabins. They were incredibly kind and very spiritual in their outlook at the clinic. I sat back in my cramped seat and smiled at the thoughts of our late night chats, our group praying sessions and the countless exchange of comforting expressions.

But a giant can of everyday problems and learned stressors were waiting for our return to the familiar. I did not know how to counter these measures or subdue their realism. I was returning to a place without the attention and love of an adoring girlfriend, which was disorientating and unusual to the last attempts. My mind therefore made it a priority. I began to think of the good and bad times that we had together and no attainable solution was offered. When we were together, she had often asked me why people would meet and love her, then slow their admiration and despise her. I never knew what to say. The honest truth was that people met her, became energized by her confidence and then

respectful of her willingness to sacrifice her popularity in order
to prove herself right at all costs. After a while, they would come
to realize that she would also sacrifice their images if they did not
comply with her own wishes or chosen argument. I decided to tell
her and every women in my life the same thing.

"Sometimes, when you win, you lose and when you lose, you
actually win," I planned to inform them with care but it was not
my role anymore. They would have to make those deductions
on their own. The heart only understands what the mind knows
through individual experience, but who was I to tell anyone how
to live?

I was only in charge of my own destinations and learning
curves. Few of the insights I had gathered actually brought forward
any helpful understandings. The glue began to melt and solidify,
shaping into a painful re-enactment of ghostly chills that left me
stained. I wallowed in those feelings until I could fight them no
longer. Hating life and everyone in it, there was a natural response
bubbling – to love myself, and everyone God put in my path. Trust
was required and I made a daily effort of screaming, "I trust you"
at my disobedient limbs. It was a whimsical attempt at trying to
mend a lifetime of distrust and fear. I have heard that every human
action is preceded by the thought, "Will this bring about pain
or pleasure?" That outcome is up to me though. The presence of
circumstance or chance only reinforces the inevitable truth, the
obvious and simple accompaniment of love in everything I pursue,
even when I do not see the wood for the trees. Concentration was
the cure in my mind, disappointed by the efforts of some people
towards me; I wondered why they did not try harder. Although it
would have made little difference, it was the attention that I craved.
Just like consoling words of a loved one or family member or life
partner. I cannot say how it happened, the daunting conclusions
that woke me up each morning. After a while, I stopped asking for
the answers. Each day, as I slipped into consciousness, the instinctive
ordering of plans took over but conclusions aren't solutions. They
are the pacifiers of troubled minds and as a trillion thoughts swim

around my conscious mind, I am tempted to abandon ship in hope of an unexpected, spontaneous end to this rubbish.

I'm almost sure that in some other place I am happy and content with my situation but in this turmoil, I am so lost in my head that I do not know what is real anymore. The road has been long and it feels as though it has left a scar on my character that will never heal, as if I crossed a line that should not be passed over when I found myself reaching for razor blades in the bathtub. The aftertaste is bitter. I peer through doorways, at people and put a plastic smile on when they interact with me. Open and honest, I speak to them as though our paths were meant to cross. But how honest can a person be who hides behind a pseudonym, especially one as ridiculous as Janji Slab?

"My name is Karl Horst … AND I AM DIFFERENT because I think in prose."

I have spent my life trying to follow guidelines, choking on the fumes caused by my own foreseeable limitations. I have hidden my face from the glare of others and apologized for my atypical name or views. The element of fear was always there and I would regurgitate the words "no pain, no gain," which was about as helpful as trying to pull a steamroller with my teeth! The truth is that clichés are flawed, conclusions change and the empathy that I, Karl Horst, experience, is mine alone. It has been said that adversity brings about depression. Not true. Loneliness is the one that carries sadness. I am comforted by so many living angels that I can't be afraid or saddened any longer. What makes me unique is that I know they are there for me. In my temple, they make me perfect. But no one is perfect. The production of results is nothing compared with the effort displayed. It is how hard they try that show their love for this odd author.

Chapter 19 Evolution

Back in our recognizable environment, an emotional storm was brewing. The treatment in Holland had brought about a mediocre 200 % improvement to my condition. We were delayed overnight in Johannesburg and stayed at the hotel lodge. The lodge appeared clean and the bed was comfortable after a long flight from the other side of the world. The novelty of being home wore off the following morning. I wheeled myself past the dining area towards the entrance to have a cigarette and to think. I was convinced that no girl would be able to love me in my compromised state.

"Please God, don't leave me alone like this," I said under my breath, "send me an angel."

Silence …

I moved in again as a group of travelers passed me on the right.

"Do you want a hand?" asked one of the members.

"A pair of obedient legs would be great," I replied without looking.

We spoke outside and while they were all very interesting, one caught my eye and I could not remove it from her pretty face. She was introduced as Riana and as we exchanged phone numbers, I remember thinking, "Holy smoke – that was fast!" We fell in love shortly after.

My dad and I traveled home with anticipation of what to expect. I phoned my friend, Malcolm, on the way back.

"I'm back, Mal."

"Welcome home, Champion. When do we open the champagne, my boy?" he asked.

"I'm not there yet, but will be soon, my friend," I assured him.

The fight at my parent's house required more than prayers although my mom had employed a very special and incredibly wise woman, named Thobeka, to maintain the house. I immediately nicknamed her 'Mama Ingilosi' (Mother Angel) when we met. Her inspiration is beyond words. But I needed to exercise every day and test the results of the cabin therapy in practice. I booked myself into a physical rehabilitation centre where I lived and worked five days a week. The people at the clinic were friendly but it was basically still in a hospital environment. Nurses and caregivers ran it with clockwork precision. I believed that the whole experience was evolving my character and prompting me to stand on my own two feet again.

Breakfast was the friendliest time of day as the wheelchair-bound patients conversed happily with each other before their stringent exercise programs began. The therapy was holistic and included doctor appointments, weekly appraisals and, of all things, psychological evaluation. It dawned upon me that, as I looked at the gunshot victims across the room, people healed there because their will to survive became stronger than their will to succeed. The resident psychologist had another interpretation, however. The fair-haired man subscribed whole-heartedly to a life-view of objectivity. He poured it on thick one afternoon in his office.

"Do you realize what could happen to you in the near future?" he asked.

I knew the answer but did not think that it was any of his business. I am, after all, not that which can be observed or dissected in a one-hour meeting. He eventually gave up on the idea and asked me to tell him of any recurring dreams that I could remember. Little did he know but he was about to learn a lesson in human defiance. I paused for a second and began to speak honestly with a straight face.

"Well, I had one dream recently," I said with an embarrassed inflection.

He started to scribble on his notepad and urged me to continue.

"It's a bit rude, so don't judge me until I am finished," I requested. "I dreamt of a man with huge testicles, so large, that when he made love to women it would cause them so much pleasure that their hearts would explode and they would die."

"What happened then?" he asked.

I lowered my head and continued, "The man had an accident and lost one of these vital appendages. The people in his hometown teased him and nicknamed him 'One-Stone'."

"What did the man do then?" the psychologist delved deeper.

"Well, he wanted revenge so he picked up two women and made love to them all night."

"Were the women okay afterwards?" he asked.

"Yes, they were fine," I responded.

The scratching of pen on the notebook paused.

"So what do you think it all means?" he asked.

"It troubled me for a long time," I started again, "but now I see that it is so simple."

The psychologist began to laugh in a way that suggested my analysis would be incorrect. I looked him deep in the eyes.

"It is obvious," I said … "you simply can't kill two birds with one stone!"

I left the office for the last time and hated being treated like a statistic.

I thought about my evolutionary process that evening. I realized that it was my path to walk alone. I discharged myself from the clinic the next day. I write the rest of this chapter with a stiff index finger pointed at you, the reader. Preparations are over. It is now time to speak of what I have learnt.

Some accepted theories are truthful. The phrase: "That person drains me of my energy," is one of these truths. A parasite is a living organism that lives within or near a living host. It feeds off the host's energy resources, ultimately depleting them completely. This is true for human parasites as well, people who thrive on the energy of others. They are not to blame, as they do not know that they are parasites. All they do acknowledge is that when they are around certain people, they feel physically better. The other people, however, feel worse. An energy displacement is present in these moments. I had a friend when I was younger who thrived off my energy. Human parasites attain or get access to your energy through the subtle manipulation of compliments and corresponding criticism in your presence. When I saw this friend from my youth, I was drained and emptied of both physical energy and mental optimism. I reached the happiest and most energized point in my life when he was not around to capitalize on my newfound confidence. I wonder where the idea of vampires first came from? My solution to the encounters with such people is simply to avoid them. They cannot feed off that which is not available to them. If you can't do that, then give them unjustified sympathy for simply being themselves. That energy is weightless.

Another cliché, which is true, comes from the saying: "Free your mind and the body will follow." The opening of one's mind to possibility, in my opinion, is enough to open the door to a set of circumstances and unexplainable outcomes. It is the single movement in the right direction and is, itself, active by nature. Everything on this planet, material or otherwise, started as a possibility. Entertaining a desired upon possibility is the most important step towards having it achieved. Everything else is implementation and eventually becomes the inevitable.

"The truth is within you," is possibly the most correct of expressions. The outside world can close in on you, thus forcing you to gaze inward because it is there that the truth lives abundantly. Breathe deeply and tread gently as getting there is another story but getting there is your story, enjoy it. Make yourself aware of the possibility that everything may work out and it is nearly achieved through sheer intention alone.

"Know thyself," is all that matters. True. This is what I have figured out about myself. Perhaps you, the reader, will identify with some of my new insights. I don't work through emotions – I feel them. I don't believe there is a God – I know there is a God. I don't regret – I reflect. I do not fear – I love. I don't hide – I am waiting. I don't apologize – I tell the truth. And I am not sorry – I am learning.

The unavoidable truth is that nothing - no person, no disorder, no bacteria, no virus, no emotion, no heartache and no worry has reign over you. Don't even entertain the idea that they even have a say in your outcome.

Most sideline viewers will immediately tell you to adopt a mindset of acceptance towards hypothetical things to come. This is usually with a realistic and negative tone and unusually void of compassion. It is helpful to acknowledge that something has happened. Failure to do so would be like negating an event that has already occurred. But if you focus too hard on that, you open yourself up to the possibility that the fight is lost. The intention is self-defeating. I let these concerns drift by like clouds of smoke. I decided to write this story that initially had no story-line. This is that story and unlike the other stories, my name is not used for effect. This is how I wish to view the world in all its splendor, its spine-chilling antiques and surprises. Its message was unexpected – even to me.

After our trip, Stuart and I spoke honestly. "I want to talk, Stu," I said.

"What's up," he replied.

I then explained. "You know you saved my life, bud," I said staring at his chest.

"I don't want to talk about it," he said.

"Well I do. As long as you know that I know, then we're cool."

"I know," he said, with a memorable handshake.

"Thank you, my brother."

Chapter 20 Karl's Story

'SECONDS GLUED TOGETHER'

My four pretty girls

Karl arrived in Thailand on 18 October 2006 and Janji Slab was not an island but he did feel like a piece that had been dislodged from the mainland.

Janji went in search of what he understood best, large floating masses, which stood alone in the ocean and created their own idea of paradise. He had frequented virtually every island recognized by a modern atlas. It was a strange time to be a twenty-nine year old traveler, odd things were happening around the globe and they culminated in world coverage to forge a ball of confusion and disbelief. The TV gave live updates on location reports, and objective commentary. An angel had reportedly been spotted in Greece on the weekend. A group of disease sufferers were re-diagnosed in Europe as being free of their illnesses, which the doctors could not explain. A prominent school in the north of England was being audited on a host of suspicions. The footage was filled with images of hysterical witnesses and tearful participants. Viewers were grateful and saddened by the fact that they were not present at any of the surreal locations when they pressed their noses against the TV screens. It appeared as though they were trying to climb into the comical and supernatural activities being presented to them. It was the point where fact and fiction collide.

"Seems like we got out at just the right time," said one of the Canadian tourists in the bungalow lounge on the island of Koh-Lanta. But not even islands were safe from the deity of the outside world. A large group of people disappeared from France and had to be recovered from Mauritius a few days later. A single funeral was even held in New York where two thousand women were inexplicably in attendance to grieve the loss of their beloved man of chivalry and romance who had died in a local tavern. Janji was not perturbed or shaken by the incidents. A large black cloud had formed over the island complementing the strange happenings. Janji had left the confines of western living to travel through South-East Asia, not sitting around and watching TV like he did back home. Janji waved the other guests goodnight and strolled through the darkness on the beach until all the sounds disappeared.

He muttered to himself as he walked further from the communal area. The moon's glare, its reflection off the water, was potent that evening. Janji moved peacefully towards what he thought was a solitary rock in the distance. He recalled the festival celebrations of the fourth night beforehand. There had been a full moon party on the island of Koh-Penang, where hundreds of visitors to Thailand had gathered to act like vampires. Janji could not remember much except for the mammoth power surge that happened that night. The sky was, at that moment, lit up by shooting stars and comets that started the stream of nonsensical events.

"Crazy days," said the rock in a voice that startled Janji in the direction of the ocean.

The night sky lit the back of Janji and the front of his assailant. It appeared in the form of a guy in his early thirties, with hair and a beard that covered his face and a bulky pair of sunglasses molded across his eyes.

"You scared me half to death, man. What are you doing out here?" enquired Janji, still short of breath.

"I don't think you know the meaning of those words. I'm just trying to get my bearings and figure out what's going on right now," said the rock calmly.

Janji slowed down and moved a few yards from the shoreline.

"Madness everywhere, hey, I'm Janji Slab."

"I'm Karl Horst," came the reply with a firm handshake after a brief pause.

Its good to hear a South African accent out here," said Janji to the outlined guy on the sand. "What part are you from at home?"

"I come from all over," told the new acquaintance to Koh-Lanta.

"Well, what brings you to this diamond in the rough?" Janji pushed deeper,

"I'm not sure, I guess I'm here to find something," he offered with apathy.

"People come here to lose things, not find them," laughed Janji, "their minds mostly."

"Maybe it's to find someone then?" riddled the bearded man.

Karl started to giggle into his chest. "Everything has a price here man. I hope you brought a lot of money?"

"I'll be fine. You should worry about yourself."

The conversation ran dry and Janji departed by saying, "See you later, Karl."

"I'm sure you will," saluted his conversational partner.

Janji walked back to his bungalow, disorientated by his meeting with the stranger.

The next day was a typically relaxed day at the resort. There were games of frisbee and sunbathers galore. The TV was put away and life was on the menu again. The bronze and gold bodies rejoiced in the thought that the outside, nervous world was millions of miles away. Janji was eating breakfast in the shaded corner of the restaurant, stopping only to throw gestures at the moving guests. The usual crew was enjoying their morning ritual. The two Danish divers were planning their next adventure into the deep blue. The Swedish girls were recovering from their escapades the night before and a tacky guy was in the centre of all the fuss, silently enjoying a milkshake and eggs. Janji moved past him towards the open exit.

"Morning, bro," Janji said with a loaded expression.

Karl lifted his head and was still sporting his large sunglasses from the night before. Janji, however, was wearing a t-shirt that said: "Why bother?"

"Hey, I wondered if we would ever meet again, what you are doing today?" asked Karl.

Janji looked around as if to try and find the answer, but it was not there.

"Don't know yet, why, what you up to?"

"I thought I'd get a picture of a triggerfish," announced the new visitor to the island with a full mouth.

Janji pulled a chair the wrong way around as he sat down with his interesting new friend.

"That's suicide. What do we need, besides big balls, to do that?" he pressed eagerly.

"Well, we got to get a small boat, snorkels, fins, a disposable water-proof camera and some of those Swedish chicks for morale."

Good, I'm only at my best when there are a group of hot girls to witness my bravery," said Janji. He waved his right hand in the direction of the girls. Vesna responded and approached the boys.

She was a brown-haired girl with a bounce in her step and a bubbly personality. After the introductions, Janji sold the idea of a group outing to the easily persuaded twenty-three year old girl. She took the news back to her companions and the five girls ran off to their rooms to get ready.

Triggerfish are feared more than sharks in Thailand. They are aggressive, territorial silver bullets that patrol the ocean floor for trespassers or vagrants. Armed with speed and scales like body armor, they ram their enemies with a ferocious velocity. Those who have seen the colorful guardians, avoid another encounter and those who did not see them until it was too late, paid the price of a serious injury.

The two men packed the boat, which was the size of a canoe and had a small Volvo engine attached to the rear. The witnesses climbed on board and took their places at the sides. The entire trip lasted thirty minutes before the vessel came to rest at the furthest point at the floating buoys. The testosterone junkies prepared to submerge themselves with only cheap cameras slung over their shoulders. The girls chuckled as they entered the water. Karl replaced his sunglasses with a pair of equally large underwater goggles.

"Lets go, bad boy," said Karl as they slid over the side. The girls seemed more excited about the descent than the guys. Janji had always loved being underwater. It also loved having him there alongside the seaweed and colorful shells. But they weren't there to sightsee. They were paparazzi for one of the grumpiest stars around. Almost everything started to appear like a triggerfish. The two snorkelers jolted around the coral walls and kept the bottom of the boat in sight at all times. They eventually ascended up to the safety of the craft and a hero's welcome after a lot of wasted energy without success. As they were inches from grabbing hold of the fiberglass, Karl motioned a distress signal to Janji as if to say 'behind you!' Janji tumbled into the boat, jerking his head around to make sure that he was not in any danger of being slammed by an angry fish. Karl surfaced with a roaring laughter.

"That's not very funny!" screamed Janji.

"Relax," reassured the practical joker.

"Don't you know what happened to the boy who cried wolf?" Janji's eyes were on fire.

"Yes, that boy feared something so much that it eventually became real."

"Maybe you should be careful about what you say and do then," informed Janji. The girls were silent at their lookout posts. Karl appeared regretful but he stood his ground.

"I do not bow down to the fear of anything, no matter how eminent. I think the wolf was affected the worst, getting accused of doing things just because he was seen as being different. We cannot get a clear view of anything if we are afraid of its existence."

"But fear keeps you alive, bro. That's how you are aware of things festering on the horizon. Otherwise we are always defenseless." ·

"Hey, my little brother," said the older man. "It's the stuff we try to avoid that becomes real. We wish its appearance upon ourselves. It's the law of attraction. If you set your attention on anything for too long, it materializes."

"How many times is too long, oh Guru?" asked an irritated Janji. The boat moved sideways suddenly as if struck by an underwater missile. The crew fell silent but Karl continued.

"Once is too long if it's accompanied by the right emotions. We are told otherwise, but it is an incorrect and upside down assumption."

The girls decided to join the conversation. "Can we go back now because we don't feel safe?"

"Don't worry girls – Nkosi Ekhona."

"What does that mean?" asked Vesna.

"It means that God is here," whispered Janji.

The boys smiled and put their difference of opinions aside, turning the boat in the direction of the shore where life was simple. The girls made small talk the whole way back. Once on the land, they scattered to discover what they had missed that day. Janji and Karl left too, deciding to meet up later under more casual circumstances. That night was the same as the ones before it. Psychedelic red and blue lights cascaded across the main beach while loud dance music urged the crowds to move faster towards a hostile awakening. A figure moved in the distance and approached Janji near the nightclub.

"Well if it isn't the Wolf," said Janji with a sneer.

Karl slid sideways but even in pitch-darkness, did not remove his ever-present dark sunglasses.

"Hey champion, you having a good time?" he asked.

"Always, why aren't you?" The conversation ran dead before Karl responded.

"I am preparing for another adventure tomorrow. How does eight-thirty sound?"

"Sounds cool, you crazy stranger. I'll bring the girls."

Karl leaned forward as if to let Janji in on a secret.

"Bring whatever you want, bro, because tomorrow we are hunting tigers."

Janji had never hunted anything except blondes, so the next morning came as a shock to the young man. Karl was waiting in the cafeteria with a fresh cup of coffee, a flamboyant new pair of sunglasses wedged deep against the sockets of his eyes.

"Good morning, Wolf!" said Janji with a croaky voice.

"Good morning, Brother. Are you ready for today?" replied Karl.

"Of course, my man, be back in fifteen minutes." Janji disappeared and prepared to round up the troops while his counterpart filled up on coffee.

The two boys and three girls arrived at Tiger's Valley later that morning. They hiked for thirty-five minutes into the stomach of the deserted gorge where tigers were once said to have roamed. The heat was inescapable that day and the members of the expedition rested in an area shaded by tall coconut trees. The boys removed their shirts, and the girls' giggling increased almost instantaneously. They, too, removed their tops, soaked them in cold water and placed them delicately on their heads. Privacy often overcomes inhibitions. Janji walked away from the group, inspired by his ego to act tough. He grabbed a loose branch and swung it like a golf club as he shouted, "Here, kitty-kitty." Karl made them immediately crave his attention again. The landscape seemed to appear forever like a blanket of moist green foliage.

"Hey, Karl, don't you like the view on this side?" said one of the blonde Swedes.

"It is very pretty over there," he said, "but I have eyes only for someone else." Karl's body position did not move as he continued: "I am lost in a dream of perfection."

"And who's in that dream?" asked the tallest of the girls.

"Someone I know who believes in fairy tales."

"That's a bit childish," she came again.

"Maybe for normal people, but I'm glad she does believe in things unseen by others because it makes her the perfect muse."

"Where is she?" cried all three girls in unison.

"She is in my dreams and there she is a dreamer, beautiful, calm and pure.

"Are you a writer?" joined the last of the girls.

"I'm more of a story-teller of how things really are – and she is my muse," said Karl

"Well, please tell us a story, but don't say things like you see her face when you close your eyes," they requested.

"Why, do you girls believe in fables?"

"I think we are starting to believe."

"That's good, girls, because you're all in one and I won't say that because it would be too feeble and untrue ... I see this girl when I blink. Besides, her story is not for now."

"Ok, but tell one anyway," pleaded Vesna.

"I can't tell a story while we wait for the brave knight," answered Karl. He leaned against the tree by his side and stared in the direction of Janji who was climbing a coconut-covered branch a few hundred yards away. A wind blew through the tropical valley before subsiding to listen closely. "I don't write them, they choose me even out here," he said. The girls appeared frustrated but sat still.

Janji walked over to the group still swinging his club.

"Hello girls, I hope you aren't still scared?" greeted the sweaty youngster. "There are no tigers in this valley," he informed,

"Yes there were," stated Vesna while looking at Karl, "you must have destroyed them with that sword, brave Janji."

"I suppose you're right," he said, "In my mind I have conquered them all. This must be an experience that people speak of when they say they have had 'a personal victory'." Karl stood up and stretched.

"Let's leave this place and get going," he suggested. The five adventurers made their way back to cool fans and comfort of the holiday resort. Each girl placed a soft kiss on the hairy cheeks of Karl as they moved to hit the showers. That evening scheduled to be the night of fun-filled masked celebrations in honor of the waterfall idol. The dark cloud that loomed over the main beach was dissolving and upset with the reshaping momentum, was tossing flares and electricity through the air.

"Hey little brother, meet me for a drink later. I think I'm leaving soon," told Karl. Janji nodded, followed the girls indoors and let them know that a storm was brewing.

The calamity started early that afternoon. The guests wore masks of all shapes and sizes to hide their natural forms. The party was set at the foot of the island's tallest waterfall located at the furthest point by the southern end. Karl and Janji were no exceptions to the bouncing, joyous crowds that were marching down the sandy roads. They followed the tribal dancers to the drumbeats where an untarnished spring poured into the ground. The sounds of Dave Matthews were dancing between the gyrating bodies. The two men, now safely behind their disguises, sat at the private tables covered by thatch-coned roofs, to speak over a few cocktails.

"You should have asked them for a more threatening cover," said Janji to his drinking partner who was muttering from behind a bright yellow chicken face.

"This is probably the most important conversation you will ever have, little brother."

What's up?" asked the confused expression of a monkey.

"I am compelled to talk with you about the path that you have before you."

"What makes you think you know me well enough to speak of such things?" The mood beneath the thatched cones had changed. Karl was not deterred.

"I once knew someone who was a lot like you, a thinker who hid behind his exterior confidence. No, that's not right. Let me earn some credibility. You loathe the sound of water being poured and hate it when other men touch your head without asking. Your father fears not doing the right thing because he was always told that he acted wrong by his mentor. Your mom is tough and always perseveres despite her hardships, which she faces like a wounded soldier. Your sister tries her hardest to avoid being consumed by the overactive thoughts that restrict you. You like to eat good food, make love, smoke cigarettes and listen to great music."

"That's everyone Wolf, I don't know if I want to have this chat."

"Well we've already begun and anyway, do you regret the things you tried that didn't work out or the things you didn't do?"

"Ok, let's hear it but you barely know me bro, besides, I have a few Buckets of Joy in me," said Janji as he signaled for another. "Koh-Pun-Kap," sang the boys to the barman as it arrived.

"You have more in you than you realize. There will come a time when this becomes obvious to you."

"Oh, really, when will that happen, oh psychic one?"

"I don't know exactly, now that we have spoken, things may have changed, but when it does, you will understand that sympathy is not empathy and gratitude is not love. You will acknowledge this in your pursuit of mermaids and angels."

"Come on, Wolf, could you be any more vague?"

"We are almost done. Our time together is coming to a close. I am telling you this because you are always searching for the answers, glimpses of resolutions that appear to you late at night but will soon come to you in the mornings. These will seem comforting but cannot help you overcome your hurdles."

"So what will help?"

"Your ability to adapt and your inability to stop dreaming will get you through just fine. There are two types of beings, those who destroy and those who create. You are instinctively the latter. Your life is full of memorable seconds, pinnacle points that will not be ignored. Trust me, one day you will understand that these seconds fuse together and make up your entire life, which is serious and joyous, scientific and mystical, attractive and heart-breaking. You have an enormous capacity to love. There was once a man who spoke of such things. He said that we should love the bad with the good and enjoy the struggles in between. The only thing that I wanted to say to you is that, although you may feel alone, even as you sit here with me, it is never the case. Stay strong, young brother."

"And what about God, genius?" questioned Janji.

"God? God is in the wind. Open your eyes and you will find Him."

Karl stood up and began to walk away.

"Come on Wolf, you can do better than that, is there nothing else?" shouted Janji. Karl turned to re-address his audience.

"You grew up with stress and criticism. Your father will appear to teach you that panic and stress are protective. You will look at them with child-like eyes. Your mother will seem to tell you, that pain and anger earn respect; she will voice this with criticism. They didn't mean to, they lied. Pain and anger earn pity. Stress and panic can only protect you from not seeing the bad stuff on the horizon or they will create it. These things promote selfish intentions. Stay out of these worlds, young brother, because you can't help them. You won't even be able to help yourself. So just love them because they love you. But if you want a cliché? Try these rare truths for size; perhaps you can have some more T-shirts made. Listen to whatever your heart says because blood is thicker than water so choose your natural and adopted siblings openly. Pure love doesn't need to make sense. Women will try and free you from yourself and you will try to save them from their circumstances. You are a thousand different characters, each one with a very unique story. Breathe deeply and stay focused. Salvation only takes a second. A determined boy becomes a man." Karl continued to exit, shouting the words: "Keep the 'sunnies'!"

Janji regained consciousness with a pounding in his head and the taste of glass on his tongue. He moved down to the foyer to try to find Karl and the girls. The walls of the hotel entrance were flooded with photographs of the night before. Janji saw a picture of himself and he thought, "Have I aged overnight?" The photo had his face superimposed on what looked like Karl's body.

"Your brother said good bye," commented one of the hotel staff members.

"He's not my real brother," expressed Janji.

"Well, he looks just like you," said the cleaner as he passed by.

Janji never understood exactly what had transpired that weekend. He packed the bulky sunglasses and did not touch them again until five years later, after his hands had gone numb on the golf course and his legs started to become heavy. It was then that Janji stood in front of a mirror, wearing them, outlined by a bright golden light that was shining through the stained rear window. He stood fast on his convictions and remarked, "OK Wolf, I see you. Let's do this!"

He was the Golden Boy again, the perfect boy with the perfect smile.

THE END

Sorry, Einstein, my mistake again. There is no such thing … as no such thing.

Chapter 21 What Now?

So the end is inconclusive. It cannot be written before it is lived out. I haven't learned all the secrets of life. That picture is just too big and no one has the energy to even try. The last three years have been a long journey engrossed with beasts and tests. I have learnt a bit more about myself as I traveled through the dark forest. My goals have changed and my ambitions have mutated. My outlook is skewed but feels right for the first time, maybe. I see wealth in friendships and love everywhere. I can be chained but never caged. And, although these pages may only be read by my loved ones, I can at least cross it off the 'to do before I die' list – writing a book, that is. As for my muse, she is part of my next escapade. I think I will name it, 'Spin the Bottle'.

No preconceptions or clichés were purposefully harmed in the making of this book.

Chapter 22

THE LAST POEM
(for Bryony)

No one knows how it feels,
To walk the edge,
Until they find themselves standing
On a thin broken ledge,
With clasped hands they pray
An undying pledge,
Until someone can see them,
Walking the edge.

Chapter 9 The Hidden Chapter

Or is it really done? A few months ago, I spoke with Veronica, a friend of mine's mom, and she praised my optimism before enquiring about motivation.

"What keeps you going?" she voiced across a dinner table on a balcony that overlooked the ocean.

"I want to see how the story ends," I said with an innocent expression. But I am the author of this story, the lead of this show, and if I don't know how it ends, then who does? I will step forward and write my own destiny the way I see it happening.

Karl Horst fulfilled the promise he had made to himself and wrote his story. The transition back to reality was not an easy one. He felt the turbulent scratch of every 'healing crisis' but he stayed strong. The mobility he had lost returned, and with it, his fame, fortune and thirst for life came back. Karl forgot the pain he had endured but remembered the lessons that he had found along the way. He looked backwards and forwards for the answer but it was not there. He knew that right and wrong were relative to whom he asked and so he moved to a peaceful place with his beautiful woman and discovered happiness – it was where he had left it ... alongside pure love.

I don't assume that it will come true, just because. Expectation is at the forefront of anything that has ever defied the odds. I have started on a new path, a fresh walkway, where I locate myself in my current position. I am here but I wish to be there and do not know how to get there. Finding yourself in a caring process releases a feeling of comfort and I am experiencing that comfort. I am wedged safely in the hands of the pattern of healing. The direction has changed. Each day is better than the one before it. The sky appears clearer and the moon is closer at night. I dream of a future that's rich and beautiful. I expect it to come true. The 'real' is what we focus our attention on. My life is re-filled with perfection, happiness is succulent and love is always abundant. With regards to gratitude, my life is non-negotiable and neither am I. My focus is not on suffering or death, it is on living happily. The process can take care of the details. Things are automatic again and my attraction to them is smooth.

"You need to be appreciative" – true. "Worrying is safe" – a false, rubbish, untrue belief!

The happiest people are the ones who turn their backs on such pointless thinking. So write, paint, sing and live your dreams.

That last cliché was hurt on purpose.

Karl Horst started healing rapidly on 18 October 2007. He wrote his story one ... key ... at ... a ... time. He sees that, with your greatest fears, comes your greatest aspirations. Karl Horst now lives in the right now. He still swears, "the book really did write itself".

Karl now takes a homeopathic remedy that works. It is pure gold.

SPECIAL THANKS TO

Mom, Dad and Cheri (my sanctuary)

Diana (my lovely PA)

Ingeborg (Gran) and Bernard, Nev and Wendy Slabbert, Topsy and Margie (my family supporters)

Nona (my angel)

Scottie and family

Stuart Doig (my life-saver)

Thobeka (my African Mama)

Greg Kenelli (my selfless warrior)

Nicholas and Teresa (my kindred spirits)

Malcolm, Bryony, Nix, Trevor, Bronwyn, Kevin, Genevieve, Stefan, Julie Shaw and Karen Miller (my 'siblings')

Greg (my Greek warrior)

Sarah, Nicky and Mishy-Moo

Alistair, Brett, Pippa (my life-long friends)

Hettie Pringle, Mr Smith, Mr and Mrs Anderson (my kind donors)

Winston Park Primary

Rotary Club - Johannesburg and Durban

MTV, VH1, 5FM and East Coast Radio (my soundtracks)

Kerry-Ann (my pretty music dealer)

The Doors, REM, The Dave Matthews Band, Radiohead, Collective Soul, Coldplay, Old Mol, Red Hot Chili Peppers, Seether (my poets)

Gary (my spiritual healer)

South African Media (my voice)

The University of Cape Town (my believers)

Juliet, Pete and Lorna Perkins

Murray, Angelique, Cathryn, Karin

Sean Knox (my new best friend)

Riana (my inspiration)

Kayla (my sweet little breath of fresh air)

Jozef, his cute sister and the entire Blaha family (my connection to the real)

Dylan (my web designer)
Claire (my photographer)
Wendy Knights (my artist)
Tania du Plessis (my editor)
Trafford Publishers
Dr Staub, Dr Russel Hopkins and Dr Wayne Dyer (my
    philosophers)
MS (my teacher)
The countless prayer groups (my 'long-distance operators')
Jesus of Nazareth and God (for answering my calls)

I LOVE YOU ALL